Making Designer Freshwater Pearl Jewelry

QUARRY

Making Designer Freshwater Pearl Jewelry

GLOUCESTER MASSACHUSETTS

QUARRY BOOKS

With a Special Section on Custom Wedding Jewelry

Nicole Noelle Sherman

First published in the United States of America by
Quarry Books, a member of
Quayside Publishing Group
33 Commercial Street, Gloucester, Massachusetts 01930-5089
Telephone: (978) 282-9590 / Fax: (978) 283-2742
www.rockpub.com

Library of Congress Cataloging-in-Publication Data
Sherman, Nicole Noelle.
     Making designer freshwater pearl jewelry : with a special section on custom wedding jewelry /
   Nicole Noelle Sherman.
          p.   cm.
     ISBN 1-59253-269-1 (pbk.)
     1. Jewelry making. 2. Pearls. I. Title.
   TT212.S54 2006
   745.594'2—dc22   2006003614
                                                                         CIP

ISBN-13:978-1-59253-269-8
ISBN-10:1-59253-269-1

10 9 8 7 6 5 4 3 2

Design by Lori Wendin
Production by Todd Fairchild
Photography by Allan Penn
Material on pages 30–32 and 34 adapted from *Making Designer Gemstone & Pearl Jewelry*.
© 2003 by Rockport Publishers, Inc.
Photographs on pages 9 and 11 courtesy of Tennessee River Freshwater Pearl Farm,
www.tennesseeriverpearls.com.
Illustrations by Judy Love

Printed in Singapore

To Arianna and Porter: The most creative people I know.

Contents

Introduction

Throughout time, people have been fascinated and bewitched by the pearl's luster, purity, and perfection. No one knows for certain when the first pearls were discovered or when they became objects of adornment, but it is clear they have been highly valued since their discovery. Pearls are found in nature in a "finished" state. Unlike gemstones, they need no cutting to reveal their splendor. This quality has enabled naturally occurring pearls to have value immediately, and it has also given them a certain mystique. In fact, the ancients—awed by the mystery of lustrous gems being created inside living organisms—thought that pearls were gifts from the gods.

Natural pearls have been featured in jewelry beginning with the earliest civilizations. Rare, lustrous pearls have adorned kings and queens, first ladies, and movie stars. Queen Elizabeth I was such an admirer of the pearl that she shunned precious stones and chose to drape herself and her gowns in thousands of pearls. The most expensive and extraordinary jewelry in the world incorporates large natural pearls: *La Peregrina*, The Pearl of Asia, The Hope Pearl, and The Paspaley Pearl are a few of the most famous examples. Pearls have the remarkable ability to bestow upon the wearer a sense of mystery, elegance, and grace.

In recent years, the beauty of the pearl has become available to all, thanks to the widespread cultivation of freshwater pearls. Cultivators have developed new techniques that produce greater quantities and varieties of pearls. These cultivated pearls are not only available in their classic round and glistening white form but in a range of exotic and beautiful colors and shapes. Stylish and breathtaking pearl jewelry now graces the covers and interiors of every high-fashion magazine. With a wide variety of shapes, sizes, and prices, pearls are not only used in classic designs but also in casual and modern ones. The popularity of the pearl has never been greater, and they are truly perfect for every style and occasion.

How Pearls Form

The formation of freshwater pearls is nearly the same as the formation of cultured saltwater pearls, with some important differences. All pearls are formed when an irritant enters a mollusk and the mollusk secretes a substance called nacre. Nacre coats the intruder to reduce irritation, and the resulting buildup of this substance forms the pearl. To culture freshwater pearls, the mollusk's shell is gently opened, and small silts are made in the mantle tissue. Live mantle tissue from another mollusk is inserted into these silts. The process can best be described as natural with some human intervention. Only pearls occurring naturally in the wild without human intervention deserve the distinction of natural; they are the crown jewels of the pearl world. Another difference in the cultivation of freshwater verses saltwater pearls is that freshwater pearls are formed in freshwater and the process involves mussels, not oysters. Oysters can produce only one or two pearls at a time, whereas freshwater cultivating can yield up to fifty pearls per mollusk. Also, most freshwater pearls are composed of only nacre covering mantle tissue, though more recently there has been experimentation with freshwater pearls formed by bead-nucleation (the insertion of a bead into the body of a mollusk).

The Japanese first started cultivating freshwater pearls in the 1930s in Lake Biwa, near Kyoto. These pearls were immensely popular and of a very high quality. Unfortunately, pollution has reduced the production to a negligible amount. Most pearls you see today labeled Biwa are not in fact from this region. China began the production of freshwater pearls in the 1970s and 1980s; however, the quality was inconsistent. It wasn't until the 1990s that the Chinese perfected the art of cultivating freshwater pearls. It has been worth the wait.

There are now a wide variety of freshwater pearls available in a lovely range of natural colors. Keep in mind, many Chinese freshwater pearls are dyed, bleached, or enhanced by radiation techniques; the value of the pearl changes dramatically when it has been treated. American freshwater pearls are also highly desirable. They are formed with the insertion of a bead nucleus and are left to form for three to five years instead of six months to one year. American freshwater pearls are also not dyed, bleached, or enhanced, and typically have more variation in their form. A wide variety of shapes is now possible due to the variety of interesting forms implanted into the mollusk. As a result, the creativity of the jewelry designer has greatly expanded.

In addition, there is a category of pearls that some call nature's accident: the keishi pearl. If a saltwater oyster rejects an implant, some of the remaining mantle tissue will cause nacre to form, resulting in the formation of a pearl. As the cultivation process is refined, these "accidents" are happening less frequently. This is good for the pearl farmers, as an oyster can only produce so much nacre in its lifecycle and hence can produce only so many pearls. Because fewer keishi pearls are being created, they are getting more and more expensive.

Different Types of Pearls

Pearls are generally divided into three categories of pearl shapes: spherical (round or nearly round), symmetrical (balanced and regular), and baroque (irregular). Most of the freshwater pearls in this book fall into the symmetrical or baroque category. In designing pearl jewelry, it is important to take some cues from nature. Certain shapes lend themselves to particular uses and some shapes are natural complements of each other. The following are examples of some of the shapes available.

Nearly Round

Coin

Diamond

Potato

Square

Offset

Button

Rice

Teardrop

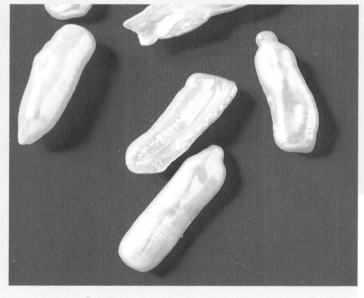

Stick

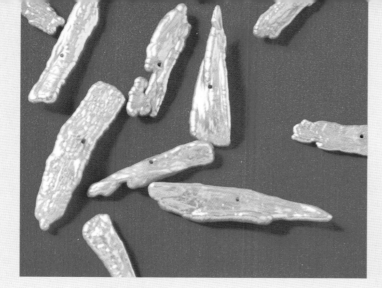

Thin Stick

Coin Drop

Keishi

Square Drop

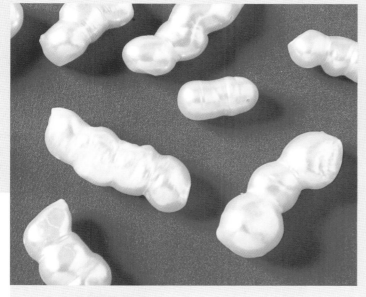

Baroque

CHAPTER 1

Getting Started

t is sometimes difficult to choose from the
enormous quantity of jewelry-making materials available today. Local craft and bead stores
have been supplemented by catalogs, jewelry shows, and the Internet. Personal preference,
cost, and availability all play a role in deciding what supplies you have on hand. The following are the basics, and the necessary components for the projects in this book. While pearls
are the dominant design elements featured here, other precious and semiprecious gemstones
can be added to create striking pieces of jewelry. I recommend spending time at a local bead
store or perhaps visiting a jewelry trade show. This hands-on approach will allow you to
become more comfortable in selecting quality materials.

Selecting Quality Pearls

The most important aspect of your design is the choice of a freshwater pearl. When I first started creating jewelry, someone told me to buy the highest quality I could afford. This has proven to be good advice. A great deal of effort goes into designing a piece of jewelry. In fact, if each piece is unique, the amount of time you spend will probably be the most expensive component of your design. By choosing the highest quality freshwater pearls you can find and finance, the finished work will be cherished for years.

The quality of a pearl is measured by seven characteristics: nacre, luster, orient, surface, size, shape, and color. For freshwater pearls, the first three are the most important; the last three are more a matter of personal preference.

An unofficial grading system applies to pearls with a scale from grade AAA (the highest grade) to C. This scale is only a guide and can be highly subjective. Finally, pearls are measured in millimeters and are typically sold temporarily strung in 16" (40.6 cm) lengths. Check that the holes in the pearls are drilled accurately and uniformly, depending on the type of pearl.

1 | NACRE

The nacre is judged by its thickness and quality. Thicker nacre is more desirable; this pertains to those freshwater pearls that are bead-nucleated, as mantle-nucleated freshwater pearls are basically all nacre. Make sure there are no cracks or peeling in the nacre, especially at the drilled hole. The quality of nacre is related to its formation. The conditions for forming the nacre must have been

Caring for Pearls

earls require special care. They are a porous, organic material that is softer and more delicate than other gemstones. Chemicals in perfume, lotion, and hair spray as well as natural oils and perspiration can dull pearls' luster. With a minimum of maintenance, however, your pearls will last for years. Apply your perfume, lotion, and hair spray before putting your pearls on. After wearing, wipe them with a soft, damp cloth to remove harmful chemicals or body oils. Store your pearls in a soft pouch or wrapped in a soft cloth to prevent scratching. You may wish to wash them periodically to remove accumulated buildup. Only use jewelry cleaners labeled as safe for pearls and only use a soft cloth. After washing, lay them out on a cloth to dry completely. Never use an ultrasonic cleaner for pearls. Finally, have your pearls restrung at the first sign of wear and have the clasp checked periodically by a jeweler.

optimal during the entire formation of the pearl for the pearl to have high-quality nacre. This quality is closely tied to the next characteristic, luster.

2| **LUSTER**

Luster is determined by the brilliance, or shiny depth, of the pearl. The pearl should not be only shiny on the surface but seem to radiate light from within.

3| **ORIENT**

The orient is the iridescent quality of the light. If the nacre is formed properly, the crystals will form a prism as the light reflects off the layers of nacre.

4| **SURFACE**

The quality of the surface is perhaps easiest to determine. The surface of the pearl should be free from blemish, smooth, and uniform in appearance.

5-7| **SIZE, SHAPE, AND COLOR**

For cultured pearls, a large, perfectly round, white pearl is typically the most valuable. For freshwater pearls, the size, shape, and color are more a matter of personal preference. In general, the rareness of the pearl determines the value.

Findings and Stringing Materials

Findings are the little incidentals required for completing a piece of jewelry. Without them, we would be left with a good idea but an unwearable one. Findings used for the projects in this book are made of sterling silver or 14-karat gold. For simplicity, I have attempted to keep to a minimum the number and variety of findings. Personal preference has a great deal to do with selection. There is a wide assortment of styles for almost every type of finding. Keep in mind that the design of the finished piece will be greatly influenced by your choices. While there are endless possibilities for creating jewelry, silk thread and stringing wire are the only two stringing materials featured in the projects in this book.

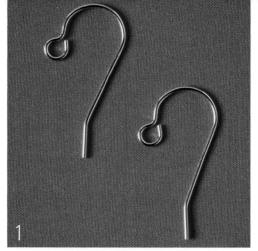

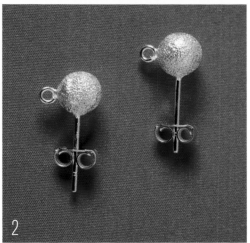

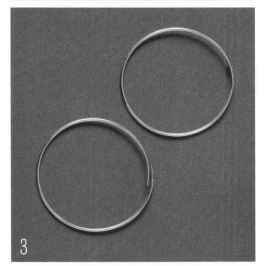

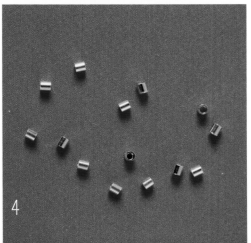

1| **EAR HOOKS**

Ear hooks are available in a large variety of designs. French wire ear hooks are used for the projects in this book.

2| **EAR POSTS**

Ear posts are the alternative to ear hooks; posts add a stylish finish to any pair of earrings. The ring attached to the post opens to allow for an added element.

3| **EAR HOOPS**

There are many different styles and sizes of ear hoops and an infinite number of designs that can be created around them.

4| **CRIMP BEADS**

Crimp beads are small, metal beads that are used to finish off necklaces and bracelets strung with stringing wire. They come in a tube shape or round bead; the tube shape is used for the proj ects in this book.

5 | HEAD PINS

Head pins resemble an upside-down nail. They consist of a straight piece of wire with a flat head on the end. Head pins are used to make earrings, dangles, or other components, and come in a wide variety of lengths and diameters.

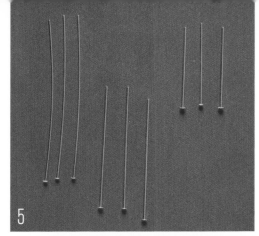

6 | EYE PINS

Eye pins are similar to head pins but have a small loop, or eye, on one end. Eye pins are used to attach a chain or can be used with a bead whose hole is too large for a head pin.

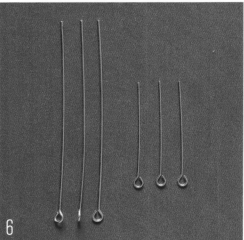

7 | CLASPS

Clasps come in a variety of designs and materials. The choice of clasp is one of the more important design decisions. Toggle clasps are generally preferred; they are easy to open and close and are a beautiful addition to almost any piece of jewelry.

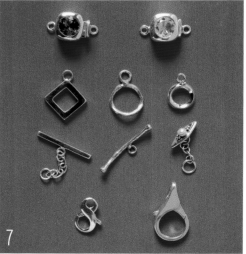

8 | CHAIN

Chain is used for several of the projects in this book. It is always popular and can be used in an amazing variety of ways. Chain is sold by the foot (30.5 cm) in different lengths, diameters, and patterns.

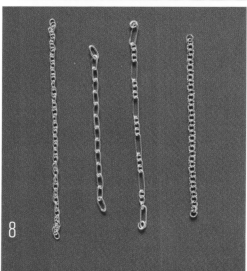

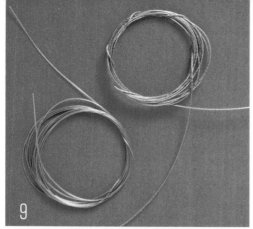

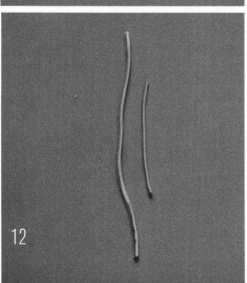

9| **STRINGING WIRE**

There are different brands of stringing wire on the market, including Soft Flex, Beadalon, and Accu-Flex. Depending on the manufacturer, there are various sizes and colors available. Beadalon is used in the projects in this book, in either a 0.018" (0.46 mm) or 0.012" (0.30 mm) diameter. The 0.018" (0.46 mm) diameter is preferred for most designs as it is stronger and less likely to break; the holes drilled for some pearls or gemstones require the smaller diameter stringing wire.

10| **SILK**

Silk thread is used for knotting between pearls. You can purchase silk on large spools or wrapped around cards with an attached needle. It comes in a variety of colors and is available in a range of sizes. Size "E" (0.0128" or 0.325 mm) is used where gemstones allow only the finest of thread, but generally size "F" (0.0137" or 0.348 mm) is preferred.

11| **FLEXIBLE NEEDLE**

This is the needle you will use for stringing pearls with silk. It has a large eye that collapses when thread passes through the pearl and is made of twisted wire.

12| **FRENCH WIRE**

Used for completing a strand of knotted pearls, French wire is a springlike coil of wire available in a silver or gold finish.

The Toolbox:
Jewelry-Making Tools

Assembling the jewelry-making toolbox can be quite fun. Feel free to clean up a vintage metal toolbox from the basement, but remember to leave the basement tools behind. While many of the tools used for projects in this book are similar to tools you might have on hand, jewelry-making tools are precision crafted. They provide a professional quality of finish to your designs. The tools you select now will affect your finished product later. While $30 (£17) might seem a lot for a pair of pliers, keep in mind that if they are properly maintained, you will have them for a very long time. Nothing is more frustrating than investing in quality freshwater pearls only to ruin the finished product with an inferior set of tools. Finally, instead of amassing a large quantity of tools, invest in a few important ones.

Beading Cloth

A variety of synthetic beading cloths are available. They are absolutely necessary in the design and creation of jewelry. Your surface must be clean and your materials must stay in place throughout the process. I prefer a beading cloth to a beading board, as it allows me more creativity in the design process (A).

A

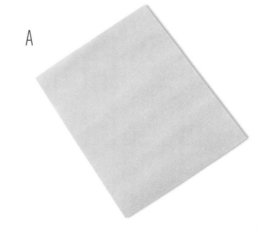

Flat-Nosed Pliers

For bending and gripping wire, flat-nosed pliers are necessary. Make sure you get a pair that is smooth and not textured on the inside of the nose; the texture will scratch your wire (B).

B

C

Round-Nosed Pliers

If you plan to create any sort of curl or loop with wire, round-nosed pliers need to be in your toolbox. These are designed specifically for jewelry making; you will not find them at your local hardware store. The tips of these pliers are cone-shaped, and provide a smooth area for curling wire to create a variety of diameter loops (C).

Flush-Cut Wire Cutters

A high-quality pair of flush-cut wire cutters is my favorite tool. While it is tempting to use the pair from the basement shop, a pair of jeweler-quality, flush-cut wire cutters cuts the wire at a 90-degree angle, enabling the end of the wire to be flat and smooth. A good pair of flush-cut cutters will reduce the amount of filing necessary, and will produce a professional piece of jewelry. To maintain the investment, these pliers should not be used for any other purpose (D).

D

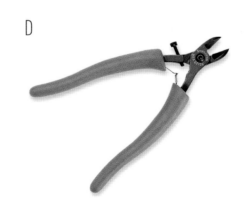

E

Crimping Pliers

Crimp beads can only be correctly attached with a pair of crimping pliers. In fact, crimping pliers are designed just for this task. These pliers have two notches in the nose that are used to fold and then press the crimp bead closed (E).

Jeweler's Files

Even if you use a good pair of wire cutters, you will occasionally need to file the ends of wire smooth. Jeweler's files are made specifically for working with metal. The files normally come in a set of six to twelve files in different shapes (flat, round, square, and half-round) and grits. Keep them in the case they arrive in; otherwise they have a way of being misplaced (F).

F

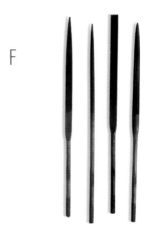

G

Tri-Cord Knotter

A specialty tool, the Tri-Cord Knotter, is manufactured by the company of the same name and is available from most beading suppliers. This tool has been designed for making the process of knotting between beads quick and easy for the beginner. Instructions for using this tool are detailed in the Basic Jewelry Techniques section of this book (see page 28) and an in-depth instruction sheet and DVD now come with each purchase (G).

Pearl Reamer

This tool is necessary to enlarge the holes in freshwater pearls. They usually come in a set of two sizes (H).

Jeweler's Cement

Many different manufacturers sell glue or cement for jewelry making. Knotted necklaces are more secure with the addition of jeweler's glue or cement. (I use G-S Hypo Cement for the slender tip at the end (I).)

Ruler

A simple tool, but necessary. You should have both standard and metric varieties in your toolbox (J).

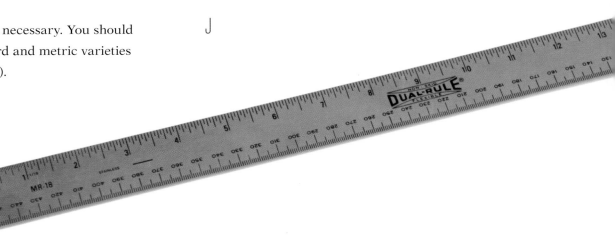

Basic Jewelry Techniques

t is amazing how many projects can be completed with a relatively small number of learned techniques. Many of the projects in this book require only one or two basic techniques of jewelry making. Wrapped and simple loops are necessary for any earring, and a wide variety of necklaces and bracelets use bead crimps or silk knots. The steps detailed in this section will assist you in the projects for this book. As you become more of an expert, you will find your own shortcuts or methods. This creativity is, after all, part of the fun.

Basic Techniques

Wrapped Loop

The wrapped-loop technique is used for a wide variety of jewelry projects. It is extremely durable and attaches the elements of your design securely. This technique is used to make earrings, add dangles to necklaces or bracelets, or make connections between different components. Be patient and practice with scraps of wire. You will want to master this skill to make perfectly round wraps without any space between the end of your wrap and the pearl or bead it contains. For this technique, you will need round-nosed pliers, flat-nosed pliers, flush-cut wire cutters, a jeweler's file, and a head pin or wire to create wrapped loops.

1| Start by using the flat-nosed pliers to bend the wire to a 90-degree angle so that you create an upside-down L shape (A and B).

2| Position the nose of your round-nosed pliers in the bend that you created in step 1 (C).

3| Use your fingers to wrap the wire around the nose of your pliers to form a loop (D).

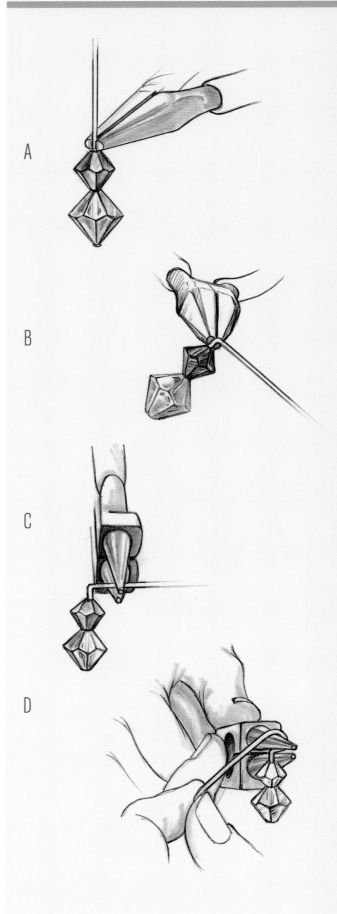

A

B

C

D

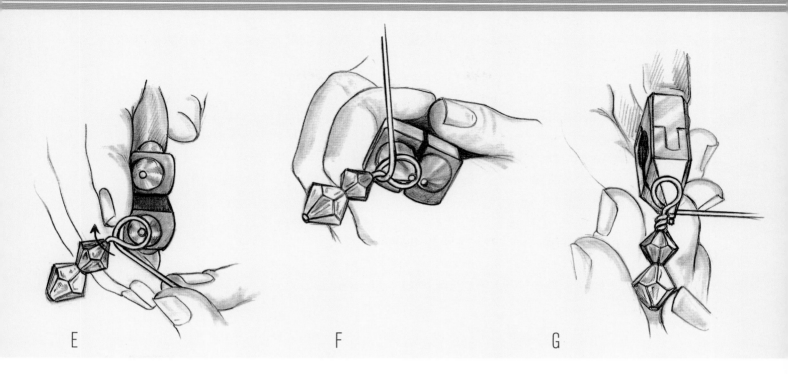

E   F   G

4| While keeping the round-nosed pliers
inside the loop, hold the loop against the
nose of the pliers with one finger (E).
You should have your round-nosed pliers
in one hand with one finger pressing the
loop against the nose. (If you are right
handed, then you will probably want to
use your left hand to hold the pliers and
your index finger to hold the loop against
the nose.)

5| Using your other hand (if you are right
handed, the right hand), start to wrap the
loose wire around the straight piece of
wire that is directly under your loop. If
the wire is soft, you can probably do this
with your fingers. Otherwise, use flat-
nosed pliers to hold the loose wire and
wrap (F).

6| Continue to wrap as many times as you
want, and, if necessary, trim off the
excess wire with wire cutters and file the
ends smooth with a jeweler's file (G).

7| Use your flat-nosed pliers to press the
wire-wrapped end flat to make sure it
does not scratch or poke.

8| If necessary, use your round-nosed pliers
to straighten the loop.

Basic Techniques
Simple Loop

This technique is a simplified version of the wrapped-loop technique. Although wrapping the wire around itself is more secure, this simple loop technique can be surprisingly strong if done properly with a thick enough gauge of wire. For this procedure, you will need round-nosed pliers, flat-nosed pliers, flush-cut wire cutters, and a 22-gauge (0.65 mm) head pin or section of wire.

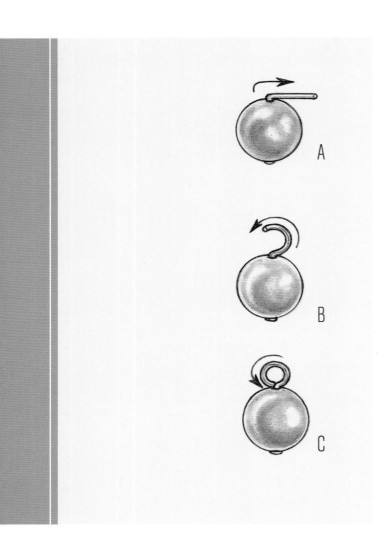

1| Use your flat-nosed pliers to bend the head pin to a 90-degree angle (A). Make sure that the part of the head pin that is bent is about ½" (1.3 cm) long, and, if necessary, trim any excess with wire cutters.

2| Position the bent part of the head pin so that it is facing away from you.

3| Then, using round-nosed pliers, grasp the end of the bent head pin and make sure that the middle part of the pliers' nose is holding the pin. Do not allow any of the wire to protrude from the other end of the pliers. This will make the end of your loop complete the perfect circle. After positioning your pliers correctly, slowly curl the wire toward you (B).

4| Because the first curl will probably not complete the entire loop, release and reposition your pliers on the circle loop you have started. Continue to curl it toward you until you have made a full circle (C).

Jeweler's Files

When cutting wire to create jewelry components such as dangles or earrings, you
may notice that the ends of your wire are
rough to the touch. These rough spots can
poke or scratch and catch on clothing. A
professional designer uses a jeweler's file to
smooth the ends.

1| After cutting a piece of wire, run the file
in one direction against the end that was
cut. Always file in one direction, never
back and forth.

2| After making a piece of jewelry that uses
wire, use your fingers to double-check the
wire areas (such as wrap loops) to ensure
the wire is smooth. If you feel a rough
spot, run the file in one direction against
this area again.

Basic Techniques

Crimp Beads

A piece of jewelry can be finished on the ends in a number of different ways. I prefer the look of stringing wire and crimp beads to nylon thread and bead tips, but it is really a matter of personal preference. Many of the projects in this book use stringing wire and crimp beads, but nylon thread and bead tips can be substituted for some of them. To use crimp beads, a pair of crimping pliers is required. In addition to crimping pliers, you will need tube-shaped crimp beads, round-nosed pliers, flush-cut wire cutters, and beading wire.

1| Slide one crimp bead onto the end of a piece of beading wire, and loop the wire back through the crimp bead after adding the clasp or other jewelry component such as a section of chain or a wrapped element (A).

2| Position the crimp bead inside the second notch in the crimping pliers (the one closest to you when you are holding the pliers in your hand), making sure that the wire has not twisted inside the crimp bead. Close the pliers firmly around the crimp bead. You should see the crimp bead now has a groove down the middle so that it curls (B).

3| Now, position the same crimp bead in the first notch in the pliers, aligning the groove with the opening of the crimping pliers. Close the pliers very tightly around the initial crimp so that you are flattening the curl (C).

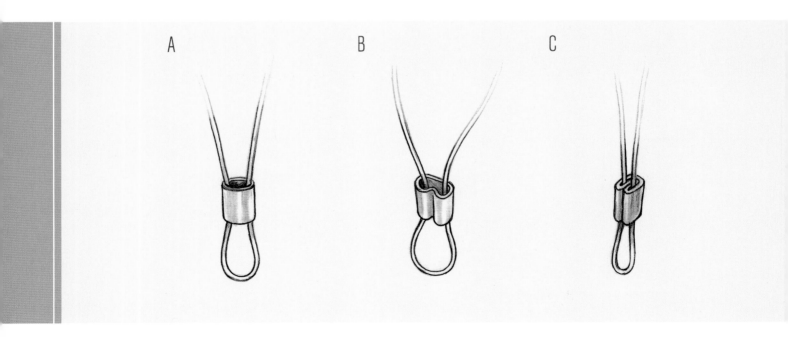

A   B   C

Reaming Pearls

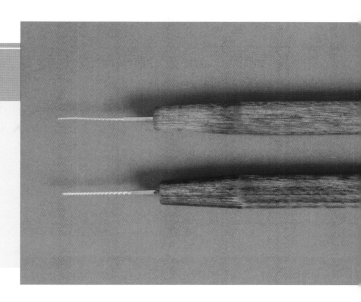

freshwater pearls are often drilled with holes too small to allow for thicker gauge wire or for double passes of stringing wire or silk. Since pearls are a relatively soft material, it is easy to hand-ream a larger hole. It is possible to use an electric Dremel or diamond-edged reamer, but with a little patience, the hand-held pearl reamer is more desirable.

4| Use wire cutters to trim off all but about ¼" (6 mm) of excess beading wire.

5| Add your pearls, making sure you slide the first pearl over both pieces of wire on the end. It is quite possible that the stringing wire will not pass through the hole in the pearls a second time. You have the choice of reaming the pearls to allow this second pass or cutting the wire flush with the end of the crimp bead. If you have crimped the bead securely, cutting it flush will not be a problem.

6| Once you have completed the stringing of your design, you are ready to finish the other end. Slide a second crimp bead onto the end of your wire.

7| After adding the clasp or other jewelry component, loop the wire back through the crimp bead, making sure it does not twist within the crimp bead, and thread the stringing wire back though the last pearl on this end of the wire.

8| Insert the nose of your round-nosed pliers into the loop.

9| While holding your round-nosed pliers with one hand, gently pull the beading wire with your other hand so that you push the crimp bead up against the other beads. This will ensure that you do not have any extra slack in your finished piece and that you also keep the end loop of your beading wire intact.

10| Repeat steps 2 and 3 to close the crimp bead.

11| Finish by using wire cutters to trim off the excess beading wire.

Basic Techniques

Tri-Cord Knotter

The Tri-Cord Knotter is made specifically for knotting between pearls. While it is possible to use an awl to make traditional knots, the knots made with the Tri-Cord Knotter will typically be more uniform and tight, saving time and much frustration. This tool takes some practice to use, but it is worth it. It isn't long before you establish a relaxing rhythm. To knot with the Tri-Cord Knotter, you will need pearls, silk thread, and a flexible, twisted wire needle.

1| Start by finishing one end of your necklace in the manner detailed in the given project.

2| String on all the pearls that will be knotted with the Tri-Cord Knotter, remembering to reserve three pearls that will be hand-tied when the other side of the clasp is attached.

3| Take the end of the strand of the recently strung pearls and hold part of the strand in your nondominant hand, securing the strand with your thumb, ring finger, and pinky.

4| You are now ready to tie a loose overhand knot. Making a V with your index finger and middle finger, palm-side down, wrap the end of the strand with the hand-tied pearls and clasp around the fingers, making a loose loop. Pass the strand through this loop, through the V made with your fingers. This will create a loose loop or overhand knot around your fingers (A).

5| In your dominant hand, hold the knotter so that your thumb is resting up against the metal lip that extends out at the top of the knotter and the pointed tip of the awl is downward.

6 | Insert the awl tip of your tool into the your overhand knot and slip the loop off your fingers. You may wish to use the tip of your dominant index finger to rest against this knot while it is on the awl. It is difficult to unknot a silk knot that has accidentally come off the awl before it is knotted tight against the pearl (B).

B

7 | With your nondominant hand, hold onto the thread that contains the unknotted pearls. Grasp the wooden handle of the knotter and push the knot and awl tip up against your pearl.

8 | Take the thread in your nondominant hand and position it in the V-groove of the knotter, keeping the thread parallel to the top of the knotter (C).

C

9 | Continue to keep the tension on the thread in your nondominant hand while you use the thumb of your dominant hand to push up on the metal lip of the knotter. This will force your knot to come off of your awl tip and rest tightly up against your bead (D).

D

10 | Remember to slide another pearl down the thread to be knotted before you make another overhand loop.

11 | Repeat this method for each pearl that will be knotted with the Tri-Cord Knotter.

CHAPTER 2

" The intention is to take a material and use it in a different way. It is a desire to reinvent and in the process make it new. "

Casual: Bohemian to Bold

Today's fashions are extremely diverse.

Trends come and go, but never before has there been such a wide range of styles from which to choose. This is especially true in jewelry, where a casual bohemian look is just as accepted as a modern one.

Bohemian is a style that has come to be associated with the avant-garde, the term used to describe something slightly different than the conventional norm. The word bohemian comes from the nomadic people who roamed Europe during medieval times. These people were originally from India and Iran, not Bohemia, which is part of the present-day Czech Republic. The Europeans called them gypsies or bohemians. Their flowing, layered, colorful clothing and elaborate jewelry were hallmarks of their style. Bohemian style also was associated with the artistic and literary community in France during the late 1800s. These artists disregarded conventional standards

of behavior and led irregular lives. More recently, the hippies of the '60s and '70s were called bohemians, as they too chose alternative lifestyles. Today, we use the word to represent a style that is unconventional, free-spirited, and open to new ideas and trends. Pearls work well with this style, as they are natural, organic elements that radiate a purity of spirit.

Boldness in fashion implies modern, contemporary, or forward-thinking design. No more of Grandma's sweater set or faux pearl necklace. The intention is to take a material and use it in a different way. It is a desire to reinvent, and in the process, make it new. Freshwater pearls are perfect vehicles for this discovery. They are ever changing and vibrant but still inherently straightforward in their form. The bold designs featured in this section are modern and innovative, and are appropriate for either casual or formal occasions.

Bohemian Hoop Earrings

These earrings evoke the spirit of the bohemian gypsy with a design centered on a large sterling silver hoop. Pearl accents dangle from sterling silver chains or are constructed close to the edge of the hoop. There are many different styles and sizes of hoop earrings available, in both sterling silver and gold. The choice of the hoop earring and adornments will lend a slightly different look to every design, but each will call to mind the freedom of the bohemian.

MATERIALS

- sixteen 3- × 4-mm white rice pearls
- four 10-mm white potato pearls
- four 8-mm white potato pearls
- six 12-mm white coin pearls
- section of sterling silver 3.1-mm belcher chain with a total of 124 links
- one pair of 37- × 1.1-mm sterling silver flat center hoop earrings
- six 24-gauge (0.5 mm) 1½" (3.8 cm) sterling silver head pins
- twenty-four 24-gauge (0.5 mm) 1" (2.5 cm) sterling silver head pins
- flush-cut wire cutters
- round-nosed pliers
- flat-nosed pliers

Bohemian Hoop Earrings

1| Start by cutting the necessary lengths of sterling silver link chain into the following increments (number of links has been used for measurement instead of inches or millimeters): sixteen lengths of three links, eight lengths of four links, four lengths of six links, and two lengths of ten links. Set aside.

2| Slip the sixteen white rice pearls onto sixteen separate 1" (2.5 cm) head pins. Start a **wrap loop** for each, waiting to attach before the wraps are completed.

3| Attach each of the sixteen rice pearl wrap loops to the sixteen lengths of three-link chain.

4| Slip the four 10-mm white potato pearls onto four separate 1" (2.5 cm) head pins. Start a **wrap loop** for each, waiting to attach before the wraps are completed.

5| Attach each of the four 10-mm potato pearl wrap loops to four of the lengths of four-link chain.

6| Slip the four 8-mm white potato pearls onto four separate 1" (2.5 cm) head pins. Start a **wrap loop** for each, waiting to attach before the wraps are completed.

7| Attach each of the four 8-mm potato pearl wrap loops to the four remaining lengths of four-link chain.

Jeweler's Tip

When you are choosing your hoop earrings, make sure the closure at the top of the hoop is not too large to accommodate the links of the sterling silver chain. The links have to slip over the end of the hoop. Some hoop earrings have prongs at the end, similar to the one chosen for this project. Simply close down the prongs with the flat-nosed pliers when adding your links and then open them gently once all the dangles have been added. This technique will also secure the links onto the hoop so that they do not slip off accidentally. Make sure not to open and close the prongs too often; like all silver, the prongs will weaken with too much manipulation and may eventually snap off.

Variation

his variation uses the same hoop earring but creates a slightly different look. Without the addition of sterling silver chain, the pearls and Swarovski crystals do not dangle much beneath the hoop earring. Only the central element is longer than the rest of the pearls and crystals. While a different palette of materials is used, the overall effect of the earring is still the same—bohemian.

8 | Slip the six 12-mm white coin pearls onto six separate 1½" (3.8 cm) head pins. Start a **wrap loop** for each, waiting to attach before the wraps are completed.

9 | Attach four of the 12-mm coin pearl wrap loops to the four lengths of six-link chain.

10 | Attach the remaining two 12-mm coin pearl wrap loops to the two lengths of ten-link chain.

11 | Thread the top link of the dangles onto the hoop in the following order: three 3-mm × 4-mm rice pearls, one 10-mm potato pearl, one 3-mm × 4-mm rice pearl, one 12-mm coin pearl attached to the six-link chain; one 8-mm potato pearl, one 12-mm coin pearl attached to the ten-link chain (center dangle); one 8-mm potato pearl, one 12-mm coin pearl attached to the six-link chain; one 3-mm × 4-mm rice pearl, one 10-mm potato pearl, three 3-mm × 4-mm rice pearls.

12 | Repeat step 11 to make another earring so that you have a matching pair.

Bohemian Necklace

The bohemian necklace is unconventional. Fundamentally, it represents a freedom of spirit and a willingness to be unique. Its shape can take many forms, but the design elements of the necklace should be as free moving as its wearer. The necklace should bring to mind the gypsies of Europe, artists, and innovators. The necklace shown uses a conservative palette of materials, but it combines them to create a most unusual piece of jewelry. This design is not your typical pearl necklace. The materials are high quality, so the necklace can be worn with faded jeans or a stunning black dress.

MATERIALS

- one 10-mm white square pearl
- one 14-mm white coin pearl
- twenty-three 5-mm gray pearls
- six 10-mm white coin pearls
- eight 8-mm white potato pearls
- nine 4-mm tanzanite Swarovski crystals
- 17" (43.2 cm) of sterling silver 2.3-mm long- and short-link cable chain
- additional 6" (15.2 cm) of sterling silver 2.3-mm cable chain for dangles
- one 14-mm sterling silver toggle clasp
- two 5-mm sterling silver split rings
- one 24-gauge (0.5 mm) 2" (5.1 cm) sterling silver head pin
- thirteen 24-gauge (0.5 mm) 1¹/₂" (3.8 cm) sterling silver head pins
- thirty-three 24-gauge (0.5 mm) 1" (2.5 cm) sterling silver head pins
- flush-cut wire cutters
- round-nosed pliers
- flat-nosed pliers
- split-ring pliers

1| The center part of this necklace is a standard 18" (45.7 cm) length. The dangles make the overall effect longer. First, cut the 17" (43.2 cm) length of link chain (this will allow for an extra inch for the toggle clasp.) Always make your cuts in the middle of the three small links. This is very important later in the project when you are measuring and attaching your dangles. Your finished length of chain should have forty large links and one small link at each end.

2| Using your split-ring pliers, attach both ends of the toggle clasp to a split ring and then to the ends of the link chain. Set aside.

3| Gather the materials for the central dangle: one square pearl, the large coin pearl, five gray pearls, and three Swarovski crystals.

4| Cut 1¼" (3.2 cm) of link chain, remembering to cut the chain in the middle of the three small links on each end. This results in one small link on each end of a section of chain, with a total of three large links.

5| Using a 2" (5.1 cm) head pin, slip on the square pearl. At the end of the head pin, start a **wrap loop**, but before you wrap it around itself, slip it onto the end of the 1¼" (3.2 cm) link chain. Complete the **wrap loop**. Push the square pearl snug against this wrap. Clip off the head of the pin and start another **wrap loop**. Once complete, this loop will be snug against the other side of the pearl. Attach the pearl and the dangling chain to the center point of the necklace. The center point should be in the middle of three short links and have twenty large links on each side. Complete the **wrap loop**.

Bohemian Necklace

6| Using a 1½" (3.8 cm) head pin, slip on the 14-mm coin pearl. Start a **wrap loop**, but before you wrap it around itself, slip it onto the other end of the 1¼" (3.2 cm) link chain. Complete the **wrap loop** and clip off any excess wire.

7| Next, slip the five gray pearls and the three crystals onto eight separate 1" (2.5 cm) head pins. Start a **wrap loop** for each.

8| Attach three gray pearls and two crystals to the top large link on the center dangle link chain. Attach two gray pearls and one crystal to the middle large link on the center dangle link chain. Complete the **wrap loops**.

9| For the six dangles to the left and right of the center, assemble six coin pearls and six gray pearls. Cut the following increments of link chain: four ¾" (1.9 cm) and two ½" (1.3 cm). These measurements are approximate; just make sure the four longer sections of chain contain two large links and the two shorter sections contain one large link. All should have one small link at each end.

Jeweler's Tip

This necklace looks complicated and does require some skill in following directions. However, it is very simple once you realize that many of the steps are the same. Whenever I encounter steps that are repetitive, I try to use an assembly-line technique. This greatly cuts down on the production time. No matter which shortcuts you choose, this design will help you become quite accomplished at wrap loops.

10| Using a 1½" (3.8 cm) head pin, slip on a coin pearl. Start a **wrap loop**, but before you wrap it around itself, slip it onto the end of the ¾" (1.9 cm) dangling link chain. Complete the **wrap loop**.

11| Using a 1½" (3.8 cm) head pin, slip on a gray pearl. At the end of the head pin, (allowing for another **wrap loop** on the other side of the gray pearl) start a **wrap loop**, but before you wrap it around itself, slip it onto the other end of the same ¾" (1.9 cm) link chain. Complete the wrap loop.

12| Repeat steps 10 and 11 for the other five dangles, including the shorter sections. You should now have six dangles ready to attach to the necklace.

13| Take one of the longer dangle sections and push the gray pearl snug against this wrap. Clip off the head of the pin and start another **wrap loop**. Before you finish the wrap, attach the pearl and the dangling chain to the necklace on the middle small link after counting three large links from the center. Complete the **wrap loop**. Repeat this step for the other side of the necklace.

14| Taking one of the remaining longer dangle sections, repeat the steps for attaching the gray pearl and the dangling chain to the necklace, but attach it on the middle small link after counting four large links. Repeat this step for the other side of the necklace.

Variation

This variation uses the same design technique but creates a very different necklace. While still bohemian in nature, it has a more modern look. The length of the necklace has been shortened to 16" (40.6 cm), and the pearls and stones are not allowed to dangle too long. They are tighter to the chain and closer together. This necklace actually uses about the same quantity of material, only in a more condensed manner. If you choose a random pattern like the one featured, you need to be careful to achieve balance in your asymmetry. I use a "cast about" method. I literally take a handful of materials and gently lay them along the length of chain in a random manner. I spread them with my hand, sweeping them back and forth. After I feel I have a good balance, I hand select certain ones, arranging them in a neater order. This randomness, accompanied by selection, gives the necklace a dynamic quality while still maintaining balance. One heavy element is balanced with a different, but similarly heavy, element on the other side. It can take practice, but remember most of all to have fun!

15 | Taking one of the shorter dangle sections, repeat the steps for attaching the gray pearl and the dangling chain to the necklace, and again attach it on the middle small link after counting four large links from the last dangle. Complete the **wrap loop**. Repeat this step for the other side of the necklace.

16 | All the dangles are now attached and you are ready to add the remaining small gray pearls and crystals.

17 | Slip three gray pearls and one crystal onto four separate 1" (2.5 cm) head pins. Start a **wrap loop** for each.

18 | Attach two gray pearls and one crystal to the top large link of one of the longer dangles. Attach the remaining gray pearl to the wrap loop of the pearl that attaches to the necklace. Complete all the **wrap loops**.

19 | Repeat steps 17 and 18 for all four of the longer dangles.

20 | For the last two shortest dangles, start **wrap loops** for one gray pearl and one crystal. Before finishing the wrap, attach both the pearl and the crystal to the wrap loop of the pearl that attaches to the necklace. Complete the **wrap loops**.

21 | Repeat step 20 to make the other short dangle.

22 | All that remains is to attach the eight large potato pearls. Slip the potato pearls onto eight separate 1" (2.5 cm) head pins. Start a **wrap loop** for each, waiting to attach before the wraps are completed.

23 | Spread out your necklace horizontally on your beading cloth. The potato pearls will be attached to the center link in a grouping of three small links. Counting the large links from left to right, the potato pearls should be attached between large links numbers 2 and 3, 6 and 7, 11 and 12, 15 and 16, 25 and 26, 29 and 30, 34 and 35, and 38 and 39. Complete the **wrap loops**.

Bold Triple-Dangle Earrings

While styles vary and trends change, long, dramatic earrings have always been popular. Chandelier earrings, large hoops, and dripping stacks of diamonds provide stunning complements to contemporary fashion. Long dangle earrings are coveted because they create drama and add a sexy element to any look. The bold earrings featured in this section are a new modern twist on this ever present style. This design seeks to reinvent the long dangle earring, in a contemporary manner, incorporating the simplicity and beauty of freshwater pearls.

MATERIALS

- two 12-mm white coin pearls
- two 9-mm white coin pearls
- two 9- × 9-mm white square pearls
- five 6- × 6-mm aquamarine briolettes
- six 4-mm round sapphire beads
- one pair of sterling silver 5-mm stardust ball posts with clutches
- 12" (30.5 cm) of 2.9-mm sterling silver triple rope chain
- six 24-gauge (0.5 mm) 2" (5.1 cm) sterling silver head pins
- round-nosed pliers
- flat-nosed pliers
- flush-cut wire cutters

Bold Triple Dangle Earrings

1| Cut three segments of the sterling silver triple rope chain to the following lengths: 3" (7.6 cm), 2" (5.1 cm), and 1" (2.5 cm).

2| Carefully open one of the loops of the stardust ball post. Attach one end of each of the lengths of chain to the loop of the stardust ball post. Each length of chain should be attached by two of the links of chain. Close the loop tightly.

3| To assemble the dangles, you will need one large coin pearl, one smaller coin pearl, one square pearl, two aquamarine briolettes, and three sapphire beads.

4| Start by taking one head pin and slide on the large coin pearl, followed by one of the sapphire beads. Start, but don't complete, the **wrap loop**. Set aside.

5| Taking another head pin, slide on two of the aquamarine briolettes, followed by the smaller 9-mm coin pearl. Start, but don't complete, the **wrap loop**. Set aside.

6| Taking another head pin, slide on the square pearl, followed by two of the sapphire beads. Start, but don't complete, the **wrap loop**. Set aside.

7| Attach the large 12-mm coin pearl to the shortest of the dangle chains, the 1" (2.5 cm) length, by threading the loop through two links in the chain. Complete the **wrap loop**.

8| Making sure the briolettes are snug against the pearl, attach the aquamarine briolettes and the 9-mm coin pearl to the middle length dangle chain, the 2" (5.1 cm) length, by threading the loop through two links in the chain. Complete the **wrap loop**.

9| Attach the square pearl and sapphires to the longest of the dangle chains, the 3" (7.6 cm) length, by threading the loop through two links in the chain. Complete the **wrap loop**.

10| Repeat the above steps to make another earring so that you have a matching pair.

Variation

here are **infinite variations** on this bold design. The look changes substantially when the lengths of the dangles are shortened. It is also possible to change the color and type of the accent stones, as well as the color, size, and variety of freshwater pearls. Further, the earrings take on a more elegant look when gold is used. This variation uses 14-karat gold, antique carnelian, and garnet squares. The only requirement is that you keep the design simple and unencumbered to achieve a bold, modern look.

Bold Cuff Bracelet

The cuff bracelet is a modern design that accentuates the natural geometries of pearl forms. Round and square pearls work best in this design, accompanied by a contrast of color. The cuff bracelet is comfortable to wear but does require exact sizing. It should not be tight on the wrist but instead hang dramatically from the wrist, coming to rest just at the base of the hand. The toggle clasps make closure possible without assistance.

MATERIALS

- twenty-one 12-mm peach coin pearls
- twenty-one 12-mm peach square pearls
- twenty-eight 12- × 2-mm red coral shards
- 13" (33 cm) 2.3-mm gold-filled long- and short-link cable chain
- two 10-mm vermeil toggle clasps
- four 4-mm vermeil split rings
- fourteen 24-gauge (0.5 mm) 2" (5.1 cm) vermeil head pins
- split-ring pliers
- round-nosed pliers
- flat-nosed pliers
- flush-cut wire cutters

1| First, cut two 6½" (16.5 cm) lengths of link chain. Make your cut in the middle of the three small links. There should be two segments of chain with fifteen large links and one small link at each end.

2| Using your split-ring pliers, attach both ends of the toggle clasp to a split ring and then to the ends of the link chain. Set aside.

3| Take one head pin and add the following: one coin pearl, one red coral shard, one square pearl, one red coral shard, and one coin pearl. Repeat six times, for a total of seven head pins.

Bold Cuff Bracelet

4| Take another head pin and add the following: one square pearl, one red coral shard, one coin pearl, one red coral shard, one square pearl. Repeat six times, for a total of seven head pins.

5| To create the fourteen central design elements, an assembly-line technique is used.

6| Use the flat-nosed pliers to make 45-degree angles, exactly halfway on the remaining wire at the end of the head pins. At each 45-degree angle, start **simple loops**, but do not complete, leaving them slightly open to eventually attach to the link chain.

7| Push the pearls and red coral snug against the **simple loops**. Clip off the head of the pins. Using your finger, create additional 45-degree angles. Start additional **simple loops**, but do not complete, leaving them slightly open

to eventually attach to the link chain. Once complete, these loops will be snug against one side of the pearl.

8| There should now be fourteen elements ready to attach to the two lengths of chain. Starting at the first section of three small links, attach one of the elements with two coin pearls to the chain. You should attach it by one of the loops you have created on the end of the head pin to the middle of three small links. Firmly close this **simple loop**.

9| In the same manner as step 8, attach all the elements to the one length of chain, alternating between the elements that have two square pearls and the ones with two coin pearls. It is important to attach these elements to the chain without the chain twisting. When you hold the chain up, all the elements should dangle straight down.

10| With the elements properly attached to one side, carefully lay this chain down on your beading cloth with all the elements facing down.

11| One by one, attach the other end of each element to the other chain in precisely the same manner you did in steps 8 and 9. Check and adjust the chain frequently as you work, making sure that it does not twist.

12| Firmly close all **simple loops**, double-checking that the loops are completely closed and will not detach from the chain.

Jeweler's Tip

There are different methods for making sure the chain does not twist when attaching the design elements. For the first length of chain, it is easiest to hold the chain in between your fingers, allowing a segment to be stretched a piece at a time. This allows the element to dangle free, making it easier to see if you have attached it properly. For the other side of the bracelet, once you have laid the project on the beading cloth with the elements facing downward, the second length of chain can be laid on top of the loops of the head pins and the loops can be attached one by one. You will find you have to readjust and re-lay the chain down repeatedly as you attach each element. The long and short cable is selected because it is easy to measure distance with this chain and to identify when the loops are properly attached.

Variation

Peacock coin pearls are substituted for this cuff bracelet. The natural hues of the peacock pearls both contrast with and complement the enhanced turquoise shards. Sterling silver bar chain is the choice for this variation. As with the long and short cable chain, the bar chain provides an easy method for measuring distance between the design elements. The bracelet is finished with contemporary square toggle clasps that echo the geometries of the pearls.

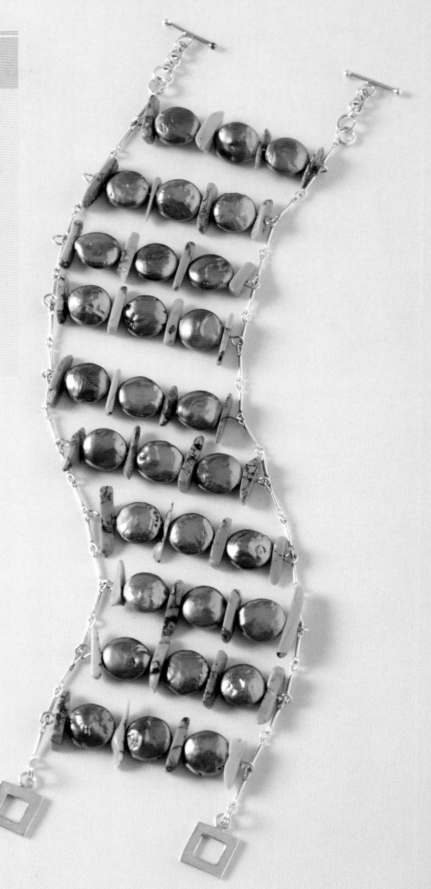

Bold Pendant Necklace

MATERIALS

- nine 10- × 10-mm white square pearls
- four 25- × 35-mm clear rutilated quartz rectangles (drilled lengthwise)
- 17" (43.2 cm) 2.4-mm sterling silver rollo chain
- four 22-gauge (0.65 mm) 2" (5.1 cm) sterling silver eye pins
- one 22-gauge (0.65 mm) 2" (5.1 cm) sterling silver head pin
- nine 22-gauge (0.65 mm) 1½" (3.8 cm) sterling silver head pins
- flush-cut wire cutters
- round-nosed pliers
- flat-nosed pliers

The lariat necklace has been updated and restyled in this design. Inherently casual, like all lariats, this necklace does not require a clasp. One end of the necklace slips through a loop of sterling silver rollo chain on the other end. Instead of being the primary material, pearls are used as accents to complement another, more dominant, material. Large rectangular quartz imparts a modern look. This elegant and contemporary lariat can no longer be identified as the traditional cowboy necklace.

Bold Pendant Necklace

1| First, cut the rollo chain in the following increments: one 3" (7.6 cm) section, two 1½" (3.8 cm) sections, and one 11" (27.9 cm) section.

2| Slip the eye of the 2" (5.1 cm) eye pin through both ends of the 3" (7.6 cm) section of rollo chain. This section will form a loop on one end of the lariat. Close the eye firmly.

3| Slip one of the large quartz rectangles onto this 2" (5.1 cm) eye pin. Start a **simple loop** on the other end, attaching it to the 11" (27.9 cm) section of rollo chain. Firmly close this loop.

4| Slip the eye of another 2" (5.1 cm) eye pin through the free end of the 11" (27.9 cm) section of rollo chain. Firmly close the eye loop.

5| Slip the second large quartz rectangle onto this 2" (5.1 cm) eye pin. Start a **simple loop** on the other end, attaching it to one of the 1½" (3.8 cm) sections of rollo chain. Firmly close this loop.

6| Slip the eye of another 2" (5.1 cm) eye pin through the free end of the 1½" (3.8 cm) section of rollo chain. Close the eye firmly.

7| Slip the third large quartz rectangle onto this 2" (5.1 cm) eye pin. Start a **simple loop** on the other end, attaching it to the remaining 1½" (3.8 cm) section of rollo chain. Firmly close this loop.

8| Slip the remaining large quartz rectangle onto the 2" (5.1 cm) head pin. Start a **wrap loop**, attaching it to the free end of the 1½" (3.8 cm) section of rollo chain before completing the wrap. Complete the **wrap loop**.

9| Next, assemble the white square pearls. Your completed necklace will have three white square pearls on each of the lengths of rollo chain, excluding the length that forms the loop on one end of the lariat.

10| Slip the nine white square pearls onto nine separate 1½" (3.8 cm) head pins. Start a **simple loop** for each, waiting to attach before the loops are completed.

11| On the end of the lariat with the 3" (7.6 cm) section of rollo chain (the end that forms the loop), count eleven links from the top of the large quartz rectangle and attach one square pearl. Close the **simple loop** firmly.

12| From this square pearl, count six links of the rollo chain and attach one square pearl. Close the **simple loop** firmly.

13| From this square pearl, count another six links of the rollo chain and attach one square pearl. Close the **simple loop** firmly.

Jeweler's Tip

For ease of use, eye pins and simple wraps are used for this project. The overall length of the large quartz rectangles does not allow for wrap loops on each end of a 2" (5.1 cm) head pin. Since 22-gauge (0.65 mm) pins are used, the simple loops should not open up and the necklace should remain intact. Of course, wrap loops will make the necklace more durable but will require longer segments of wire. Refer to the techniques section on cutting and finishing off sterling silver wire.

Variation

rutilated green quartz is used as the focal point for this bold pendant necklace. For this design, freshwater pearls are used as accents, instead of as the main design elements. Round African trade beads add color and weight to the ends of the cable chain. The length of this necklace is long enough so that is can be easily slipped over the wearer's head, maintaining a casual look.

14| On the other end of the lariat, the end that starts with the large quartz rectangle constructed with a wrap loop, count fourteen links from the top of the large quartz rectangle and attach one square pearl. Close the **simple loop** firmly.

15| From this square pearl, count six links of the rollo chain and attach one square pearl. Close the **simple loop** firmly.

16| From this square pearl, count another six links of the rollo chain and attach one square pearl. Close the **simple loop** firmly.

17| Proceeding further up the length of necklace, between the second and third large quartz rectangles, count eleven links from the top of the second large quartz rectangle and attach one square pearl. Close the **simple loop** firmly.

18| From this square pearl, count six links of the rollo chain and attach one square pearl. Close the **simple loop** firmly.

19| From this square pearl, count another six links of the rollo chain and attach one square pearl. Close the **simple loop** firmly.

CHAPTER 3

"Times change, and the cultivation of freshwater pearls has allowed everyone to be able to afford a classic."

Classic: Simple and Elegant

Classic means timeless. Classic means having long-lasting significance or an acknowledged worth. It is the opposite of trendy. It is important. In fashion, it is defined by the elegance of Audrey Hepburn or Grace Kelly. Classic is the clutch handbag, the scarf, and the black pump. Classic is the pearl necklace. The single-strand knotted cultured pearl necklace epitomized the traditional. It was the choice for brides, for wedding anniversaries, and especially for royalty. It was a wonderfully extravagant gift. Times change, and the cultivation of freshwater pearls has allowed everyone to be able to afford a classic. While some pearls are still knotted and affixed to posts, the freshwater pearl allows for much greater flexibility. Varying shapes of pearls can be combined to create lasting treasures that will one day be timeless classics.

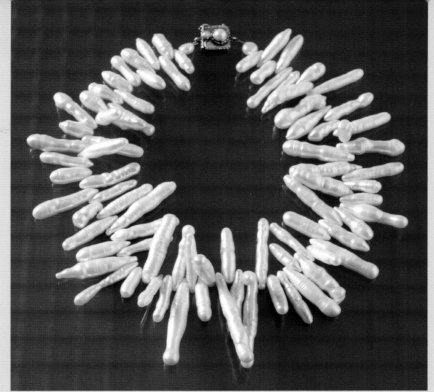

Classic Post-and-Drop Earrings

The assorted earrings featured for this project are easy to make. As the variety of freshwater pearls and their combinations are endless, so are the possibilities of earrings. Classic earrings should be simple, straightforward designs. They are sophisticated and refined. Classic earrings are appropriate for the office, church, luncheons, or just about any occasion. Stardust posts are used, in both sterling silver and 14-karat gold; they add elegance to the pearls.

1 | Slide one coin pearl onto a head pin.

2 | Using the flat- and round-nosed pliers, create a **wrap loop**.

3 | Carefully open the loop of the stardust ball post, slip on the wire loop of the head pin, and close tightly.

4 | Repeat the above steps to make another earring so that you have a matching pair.

MATERIALS

- two 10-mm peach coin pearls
- two 14-karat gold 5-mm stardust ball posts with clutches
- two 24-gauge (0.5 mm) 1" (2.5 cm) 14-karat gold head pins
- round-nosed pliers
- flat-nosed pliers
- flush-cut wire cutters

Variations

the peacock teardrop pearls used for this earring complement almost any style. The alternating pattern of the pearls gives them a modern look. It is important to remember to keep the pearls snug against each other when completing the wrap loop.

length does not alter the sophistication of these earrings. While longer than the traditional earring, coin pearls, nugget pearls, emeralds, and citrine combine to make a timeless statement.

the two pairs of earrings in this variation show that a refined look is still possible when using some of the more dynamic pearl shapes. Stick pearls of varying widths are combined with simple white coin pearls. These earrings are unusual while still being classic.

Single-Strand Knotted Necklace

A single strand of knotted, cultured pearls has epitomized the traditional necklace. It has been given to celebrate birthdays, bat mitzvahs, confirmations, graduations, and weddings. It is the sought-after gift for the thirtieth wedding anniversary. This project uses the classic technique of knotting between pearls but chooses a variety of freshwater pearl shapes to update the look. Knotting is easily accomplished with some practice and the right tool. The technique is explained in detail on page 36. The finished result will be a timeless piece of jewelry with a contemporary twist.

1| Lay out twenty-eight graduated coin pearls on your beading cloth or board, carefully selecting the sizes as you place them.

2| Insert the stick pearls between the coin pearls to create the following pattern from right to left in a clockwise manner: three coin, one stick, one coin, one stick, one coin, one stick. Repeat this pattern four more times and finish the pattern with the last three coin pearls.

3| Make a knot at one end of the silk thread and attach a flexible needle to the other.

MATERIALS

- twenty-eight graduated 10-mm to 12-mm peach coin pearls
- fifteen 8- × 22-mm peach stick pearls
- 42" (106.7 cm) of 0.0137" (0.348-mm) white silk thread
- one flexible stringing needle
- ½" (1.3 mm) of gold French wire
- one 14-mm 14-karat gold toggle clasp
- Tri-Cord Knotter
- flush-cut wire cutters

Single-Strand Knotted Necklace

4| Thread the third, second, and first coin pearl in this order and slide them to the end of the silk thread. You will need to thread the pearls in the reverse order that they will end up on your finished necklace, as you will again pass through the pearls with your thread in steps 7 and 8. This small detail makes a big difference when your pearls are graduated in size.

5| Cut the ½" (1.3 cm) French wire in half, sliding half of it onto the needle, holding the French wire between your thumb and forefinger as it goes over the needle. Slide it down the thread until it is 2" (5.1 cm) above the three pearls.

6| Slide on the bar end of the toggle clasp and push down to the French wire.

7| Pass the needle through the closest pearl in the opposite direction, creating a loop of French wire snug against the pearl. Leave the 2" (5.1 cm) of space between this pearl and the next. Hand-tie a knot snug against the pearl.

8| Pass the needle through the next pearl and hand-tie another knot. Pass the needle through the final pearl; do not knot. Leave the short tail of thread with the knot in the end dangling from the strand of pearls. This will be trimmed at the end.

9| String the remaining pearls following the pattern laid out on the beading cloth.

10| Using the Tri-Cord Knotter, make a secure knot between each pearl. Refer to the techniques section, page 36, for a description on how to use the Tri-Cord Knotter.

11| String on the remaining three coin pearls with the smallest at the end.

12| Thread on the remaining half of the French wire, followed by the round end of the toggle clasp.

13| Pass the needle through the pearl closest to the French wire in the opposite direction, forming a loop of French wire next to the pearl. Make sure the three pearls are close together, allowing only for spaces for the hand-tied knots.

14| Hand-tie a knot around the thread in the first gap.

15| Pass the needle through the next pearl and hand-tie another knot around the thread in the second gap.

16| Pass the needle through the third coin pearl. Trim off the excess thread, pulling slightly on the thread to allow the thread to disappear within the pearl when it is trimmed.

17| Trim the excess thread at the other end in the same manner.

18| Place a very small drop of jeweler's cement on the hand-tied knots at both ends. Set aside until dry.

Jeweler's Tip

Depending on the size of the hole in the pearl, you may need to ream the six coin pearls at the ends of the necklace to allow for two passes of the silk thread. Refer to the techniques section, page 35, for the proper way to ream pearls.

Variation

t **this variation uses** the same technique with a different palette of materials. You can vary the pearl shapes and colors to achieve a wide variety of effects. The gray and white pearls alternate in a classic fashion, but the pattern changes slightly, creating a modern and dynamic necklace. A large silver square toggle completes the look.

Double-Wrapped Necklace

T his necklace can be worn in two ways to achieve two very different looks. The simple layering of the strands creates a more modern and classical look, dynamic in its ability to move with the wearer. The necklace can also be wrapped by gently twirling both strands together until they are tightly interwoven. Since the strands are of contrasting colors, the effect is striking. The combination of white and gray is both classic and timeless.

MATERIALS

- eighty-five 10-mm white teardrop pearls
- ninety-four 8-mm peacock or gray teardrop pearls
- 40" (101.6 cm) nylon coated stainless steel stringing wire Beadalon 49 strand: 0.018" (0.46 mm) diameter
- four 3-mm sterling silver crimp beads
- one 12-mm sterling silver square toggle clasp
- crimping pliers
- flush-cut wire cutters

Double-Wrapped Necklace

1. Cut two 20" (50.8 cm) lengths of stringing wire.

2. Slip one end of the beading wire through one of the crimp beads. Add the square part of the toggle and slip the beading wire back through the crimp bead. **Secure crimp** tightly and trim any excess wire flush against the crimp bead.

3. Add all eighty-five of the white teardrop pearls.

4. Make sure the teardrop pearls are snug against each other without being so tight they will not form a nice circle. The teardrop pearls will rest against one another in an alternating manner.

5. Finish off this strand of the necklace by adding another other crimp bead. Slip the bar part of the toggle onto the wire and pass the wire back through the crimp bead. Making sure the pearls have not loosened, snug the crimp against the last pearl, and **secure crimp**. Trim off any excess wire flush with the end of the crimp bead.

6. Repeat steps 2 through 5 with the peacock-colored pearls.

Jeweler's Tip

One set of pearls may be longer than the other even if they are the same diameter. Pearls are organic and some variation exists. If this is the case, having an equal number of pearls may not lead to perfectly matched lengths of necklace. In this design, the strands can be wrapped as well as layered on top of each other. If they are wrapped, both strands must be exactly the same length. A few extra pearls may have to be added to one of the strands to achieve this effect.

Variation

this necklace features white diamond-shaped freshwater pearls accented with sapphires and small button-shaped pearls. The white and gray button-shaped pearls are drilled in an offset manner, which adds an additional interesting geometry to the design. This necklace is called Layered Shapes and is best worn with the strands simply layered on top of one another. It is possible to twist the strands together, but the sapphires show best when draped against the field of white diamond-shaped pearls.

CHAPTER 4

" These shapes, when combined with a strong
sense of design, can create jewelry that
can be appreciated as art. "

Unusual: Organic and Geometric

The most exciting aspect of using freshwater
pearls is the availability of a large variety of interesting shapes. These shapes, when combined with a strong sense of design, create jewelry that can be appreciated as art. Elongated pearls, baroque pearls, and geometrically shaped pearls lend themselves to different styles of necklaces, bracelets, and earrings. What is appropriate for one piece is not always appropriate for another. Spend time thinking about what makes each shape unique. This is a good way to start working on any design. The goal is to create a distinctive piece of wearable art that is not easily reproduced. The difficulty in reproduction is not a technical issue but rather a function of the innovation and individuality of its creation.

Stick Pearl Bracelet

Dynamic in design and shape, this bracelet is flexible enough to be worn at the office or to an elegant dinner party. The stick pearl is a fun shape as it is never static. The pearls flip around each other, while still being comfortable on a wrist. The accent stones add color and dimension to the white field of freshwater pearls. While requiring specific sizing, the toggle clasp is used to allow the wearer to clasp without assistance.

1| Assemble all the accent stones for the bracelet.

2| Slip six emeralds and six pearls onto twelve separate head pins. In an assembly-line manner, start and complete **wrap loops** for all the accent stones and pearls. Set aside until you are ready to add them onto your stringing wire.

MATERIALS

- thirty-three 5- × 24-mm white stick pearls
- six 10-mm rough cut irregular-shaped emeralds
- six 11-mm peacock coin pearls
- 10" (25.4 cm) nylon coated stainless steel stringing wire Beadalon 49 Strand: 0.018" (0.46 mm) diameter
- two 2-mm sterling silver crimp beads
- twelve 1" (2.5 cm) 24-gauge (0.5 mm) sterling silver head pins
- one 10- × 10-mm sterling silver square toggle clasp
- round-nosed pliers
- flat-nosed pliers
- crimping pliers
- flush-cut wire cutters

Stick Pearl Bracelet

3| Attach one end of the toggle clasp to your stringing wire with a crimp bead. **Secure crimp** and trim off any excess wire flush with the crimp bead.

4| Slip three stick pearls onto the beading wire, followed by one of the peacock coin pearls. Add two more stick pearls, followed by one of the rough emerald accents. Do not worry which side of the stick pearls the accents are on; they will change sides repeatedly once the bracelet is assembled.

5| Repeat the pattern in step 4 six times.

6| Finish the bracelet pattern by adding the three remaining stick pearls.

7| Attach the unfinished end to the other end of the toggle clasp with a crimp bead. Before crimping, be careful to have the stick pearls and the accent stones snug against each other without making the bracelet so tight that it does not comfortably form a circle around the wrist. **Secure crimp** and trim off any excess wire flush with the crimp bead.

Variation

bronze stick pearls are used in this variation. This rich hue requires a different palette of materials. There are numerous options, including bold combinations of colors, such as red and black, as well as subtler combinations of different shapes of white pearls. This bracelet uses two sizes of warm white coin pearls for contrast and two sizes of sponge coral squares that harmonize well with the bronze stick pearls. A gold toggle clasp finishes off the bracelet.

Round Drop Pearl Necklace

The luster and quality of these coin drop pearls are enough to create a remarkable piece of jewelry. They are different from the typical coin pearl, as they have the addition of extra nacre, drilled to allow innovative stringing. The way they rest together creates a vibrant necklace. The aquamarine faceted teardrops catch the light and radiate a luminosity that further accentuates the pearl's natural luster.

MATERIALS

- fifty-one 13-mm white coin drop pearls
- thirty-eight 5- × 10-mm aquamarine faceted teardrops
- two 3-mm sterling silver crimp beads
- 20" (50.8 cm) nylon coated stainless steel stringing wire Beadalon 49 Strand: 0.018" (0.46 mm) diameter
- one 12- × 12-mm sterling silver white topaz clasp
- crimping pliers
- flush-cut wire cutters

Round Drop Pearl Necklace

1| Slip one end of the beading wire through one crimp bead. Attach to one end of the clasp and slip the beading wire back through the crimp bead. Next, **secure crimp** tightly and trim off any excess wire flush against the crimp bead.

2| For this necklace, you will have three coin drop pearls at each end, closest to the clasp. The remaining pattern will have five coin drop pearls separated by either three or five aquamarine teardrops. Make sure the most perfect and uniform coin drop pearls, in terms of luster and quality, are located in the center of the necklace.

3| The pattern for the necklace is as follows: three coin drop pearls, three aquamarine teardrops, five coin drop pearls, five aquamarine teardrops, five coin drop pearls, three aquamarine teardrops, five coin drop pearls, three aquamarine teardrops, five coin drop pearls, five aquamarine teardrops, five coin drop pearls, five aquamarine teardrops, five coin drop pearls, three aquamarine teardrops, five coin drop pearls, three aquamarine teardrops, five coin drop pearls, five aquamarine teardrops, five coin drop pearls, three aquamarine teardrops, three coin drop pearls.

4| Slide on another crimp bead to finish the necklace. Slip the other end of the box clasp onto the wire and pass the wire back through the crimp bead. Before you crimp this bead, take extra care that all of your coin drop pearls and aquamarine teardrops are snug against each other. This will cause them to rotate slightly, fanning out like a pinwheel.

5| Making sure to maintain this tension, snug the crimp against the last pearl and **secure crimp**. Trim off any excess wire flush with the end of the crimp bead.

Jeweler's Tip

The unusual shape of the pearls in this design requires a bit more attention when stringing. Discard any that are drilled too close to an edge. These tenuous holes are more liable to break off with wear. Also look for any other improperly drilled holes, such as those holes that pass in and out of the pearl more than once. If strung, these pearls would allow the wire to show. Lastly, when stringing, pay close attention to the size of the edge of the pearl that will be attached. These pearls are not uniform; some of the pearls have small edges and others wider ones. If you do not vary the width of them, you will be left with a visible difference in the size of the sections of pearls. They are meant to be uniform and symmetrical.

Variation

the keishi pearls used in this necklace are often called petal pearls. Their organic shape bears a resemblance to petals from a delicate flower. They are light as air and when worn give the feeling of being enveloped by nature. The lustrous pearls used in this necklace are delicate and must be treated with care. Rubies and gold filigree accent beads combine to create an opulent piece of jewelry. A large 14-karat gold toggle clasp finishes off the look, adding another level of sumptuousness to a necklace that will be admired for years to come.

Extravagant Peacock Pearl Multistrand Necklace

There are occasions when only the most
special necklace will suffice. A wedding
anniversary, a corporate dinner, and even
your high school reunion are just a few
times when a spectacular piece of jewelry
is required. This necklace uses a generous
number of strands of peacock coin freshwater pearls. These pearls are combined with
high-quality amethyst briolettes that complement the iridescent colors in the pearls.
Finally, a strand of graduated sapphires adds
sparkle and luxury to the design.

1| Cut five 20" (50.8 cm) lengths of Beadalon
stringing wire.

2| To three of the lengths of stringing wire,
add thirty-seven peacock coin pearls. Set
aside.

3| To one strand of stringing wire, add
twenty-three peacock coin pearl, followed
by twelve amethyst briolettes and nine
peacock coin pearls. Set aside.

MATERIALS

- five 16" (40.6 cm) strands of temporarily strung 10-mm peacock coin pearls
- one 16" (40.6 cm) strand of temporarily strung 1- to 2-mm graduated sapphire beads
- twenty-one 6- × 6-mm amethyst faceted briolettes
- 100" (254 cm) nylon coated stainless steel stringing wire Beadalon 49 Strand: 0.018" (0.46 mm) diameter
- 20" (50.8 cm) nylon coated stainless steel stringing wire Beadalon 19 Strand: 0.012" (0.3 mm) diameter
- one 12-mm sterling silver amethyst three-strand box clasp
- ten 2-mm sterling silver crimp beads
- two 1-mm sterling silver crimp beads
- crimping pliers
- flush-cut wire cutters
- flat-nosed pliers

Extravagant Peacock Pearl Multistrand Necklace

4| To the fifth strand of stringing wire, add peacock coin pearls and amethyst briolettes in the following order: eight peacock coin pearls, three amethyst briolettes, three peacock coin pearls, six amethyst briolettes, twenty-two peacock coin pearls. Set aside.

5| Take the thinner strand of stringing wire (19 Strand: 0.012" [0.3 mm] diameter) and add all the graduated sapphires, making sure the largest is in the center of the strand.

6| Slip a crimp bead onto one of the strands with only peacock coin pearls, attach this to the lower ring of the multistrand clasp, **secure crimp**, and trim off any excess wire flush with the crimp bead.

7| Slip a crimp bead onto the other end of this strand, attaching to the lower ring of the other part of the multistrand clasp. Again, **secure crimp** and trim off any excess wire.

8| Repeat steps 6 and 7 for the other two strands with only peacock coin pearls, attaching to the middle and top rings of the multistrand clasp. Be careful to attach the ends to the opposing ring on both sides. For example, if you are attaching to the middle ring on one side, attach to the middle ring on the other.

9| Take the strand with twelve amethyst briolettes and attach with crimp beads to the topmost rings on the box clasp. Before finishing the crimp, make sure all the briolettes are snug against each other, alternating in directions. **Secure crimps**.

10| Take the strand with a total of nine amethyst briolettes and attach with crimp beads to the bottom-most rings on the box clasp. Again, before finishing the crimp, make sure all the briolettes are snug against each other, alternating in directions. **Secure crimps**.

11| Finally, take the strand of graduated sapphires and attach with the 1-mm crimp beads to the middle ring of the box clasp. With the flat-nosed pliers, **secure crimps**, making sure to crimp very tightly.

Jeweler's Tip

The most difficult part of designing a multistrand necklace is making sure that when clasped, the strands all lie within each other, nesting together. There should not be any long strands, or short ones, lying away from the group. This takes practice and until you get the hang of it, it is best not to finish off the ends until you are certain it will lie properly.

Matching Peacock Pearl Earrings

While pearl stud earrings can complement many freshwater pearl necklaces, some designs require that matching earrings be created. As a general rule, only the materials used in the necklace should be used for the earrings. This matching pair is the exception. Small round pearls are added to allow the sapphire beads to lie straight. The shape of the amethyst briolettes would cause the sapphire beads to lie at an angle if the round pearls were not added to the design.

1| Slide one peacock coin pearl followed by two amethyst briolettes onto one head pin.

2| Add one of the 2-mm small round pearls.

3| Finally, add two of the 2-mm sapphires.

4| Making sure the pearls and briolettes are snug against each other, use the flat- and round-nosed pliers to create a **wrap loop**.

5| Carefully open the loop of the stardust ball post, slip on the wire loop of the head pin, and close tightly.

6| Repeat the above steps to make another earring so that you have a matching pair.

MATERIALS

- two 10-mm peacock coin pearls
- four 6- × 6-mm amethyst briolettes
- two 2-mm small round gray pearls
- four 2-mm sapphire beads
- one pair of sterling silver 5-mm stardust ball posts with clutches
- two 24-gauge (0.5 mm) 2" (5.1 cm) sterling silver head pins
- round-nosed pliers
- flat-nosed pliers
- flush-cut wire cutters

CHAPTER 5

" Pearls have traditionally been associated with
marital vows. They represent purity and love. "

Weddings: Bride and Bridal Party

Weddings are a joyous time that should be filled with love, hope, and understanding. They are the gift we give each other in celebration of a life to come. Unfortunately, they are also filled with endless decisions, some of which can produce great anxiety. Having a carefully chosen idea for the jewelry for the wedding party is essential and can eliminate some of these concerns. Pearls have traditionally been associated with marital vows. They represent purity and love. The first mention of pearls and weddings goes back to 1000 BC with a Hindu story of a father who "brought forth pearls from the depths of the sea to give to his daughter on her wedding day."[1] In the romantic stories of the Middle Ages, it was the knight who returned with pearls for his lady as a treasure to be bestowed on her for her wedding day.[2] This tradition continues today, with pearls being the most popular choice for adorning the bride on her special day.

The variety and accessibility of freshwater pearls makes it possible for brides not to be the only recipients of beautiful strands of pearls. The entire wedding party can enjoy pearl jewelry. This has the added benefit of coordinating another layer of the wedding. Dresses and flowers are important, but the jewelry should not be overlooked. A wedding is a memorable event, a milestone in one's life. There is nothing that better symbolizes this occasion than the luster and beauty of pearls.

1, 2: *The Pearl Book: The Definitive Buying Guide How to Select, Buy, Care for and Enjoy Pearls.* Antoinette Matlins, P.G., Gemstone Press, Woodstock, Vermont, 2005, Third Edition

Coin Pearl and Aquamarine Bridesmaid Earrings

Often a bride has many bridesmaids.

These beautiful, individualized earrings are a great way to thank your bridesmaids and ensure gorgeous wedding photographs. Many wedding pictures are compromised by too much diversity in the choice of jewelry in the wedding party. The simplicity of this earring can accent rather than detract from whatever the bride chooses for her necklace and earrings. The other real advantage of this design is it can be easily varied to provide numerous similar, yet unique, pairs of earrings. This lets each bridesmaid know she is special. One way to personalize the earring is to vary the accent stone based on the bridesmaid's birth date. Refer to the chart (page 92) to determine which stone is appropriate.

MATERIALS

- two 10-mm white coin pearls
- three 6-mm aquamarine briolettes
- two 20-gauge (0.8 mm) sterling silver French wire earring hooks
- two 24-gauge (0.5 mm) 2" (5.1 cm) sterling silver head pins
- round-nosed pliers
- flat-nosed pliers
- flush-cut wire cutters

Bridesmaid Earrings

1| Slide a coin pearl onto one head pin. Follow this with the three briolettes that correlate to the bridesmaid's birth date.

2| Making sure the briolettes are snug against the pearl, use the flat- and round-nosed pliers to create a **wrap loop** on the end of the eye pin. Either slip this wrap loop on the ear hook before wrapping the wire around itself or carefully open the ear hook in a sideways manner and close after the wrap loop has been added.

3| Repeat the above steps to make another earring so that you have a matching set.

Jeweler's Tip

When adding briolettes to a design, ideally all the briolettes should be the same size. If the briolettes are differing sizes, they can be arranged with the largest in the middle surrounded by two smaller, equal-sized ones. They can also be arranged in ascending order, with the smallest at the top and the largest at the bottom, next to the coin pearl.

BIRTHSTONE CHART

There are many lists of birthstones. Columns two and three contain the traditional and modern birthstones, as adopted by the American National Association of Jewelers. The last column shows the more informal list of birthstones by the zodiac.

MONTH	TRADITIONAL	MODERN	ZODIAC	DATES	STONE
January	Garnet	Garnet	Aquarius	Jan 21 — Feb 18	Garnet
February	Amethyst	Amethyst	Pisces	Feb 19 — Mar 20	Amethyst
March	Bloodstone	Aquamarine	Aries	Mar 21 — Apr 20	Bloodstone
April	Diamond	Diamond	Taurus	Apr 21 — May 21	Sapphire
May	Emerald	Emerald	Gemini	May 22 — Jun 21	Agate
June	Alexandrite	Pearl or Moonstone	Cancer	Jun 22 — Jul 22	Emerald
July	Ruby	Ruby	Leo	Jul 23 — Aug 23	Onyx
August	Sardonyx	Peridot	Virgo	Aug 24 — Sep 22	Carnelian
September	Sapphire	Sapphire	Libra	Sep 23 — Oct 23	Chrysolite, Aventurine
October	Tourmaline	Opal or Tourmaline	Scorpio	Oct 24 — Nov 22	Beryl
November	Citrine	Yellow Topaz or Citrine	Sagittarius	Nov 23 — Dec 21	Topaz
December	Zircon, Lapis Lazuli	Turquoise, Blue Topaz, or Tanzanite	Capricorn	Dec 21 — Jan 20	Ruby

Variations

t **hese bridesmaid earrings** can be varied in many ways. As suggested in the introduction to this section, deviations can be based on the birthstones of the bridesmaids. Additionally, it is possible to vary the earring for the maid of honor by using slightly larger briolettes, as shown here in citrine. Citrine is both the modern and traditional November birthstone.

I **t is also possible to use** different shapes of pearls to make distinct earrings for each bridesmaid: coin, square, and stick. A word of caution: Varying the color of the briolettes *and* the shapes of the pearl can appear too busy in wedding photographs. A varying pearl shape works best if all the briolettes are the same, as shown here in aquamarine. Varying the pearl shape and not the color of the stone might be considered if the stone is to coordinate with the color of the bridesmaid dresses. This is another approach to personalizing the earrings while still maintaining harmony in the selection of jewelry for the wedding party.

Maid of Honor Pearl and Gemstone Bracelet

The role of the maid of honor can be one of
the most important in a wedding. She is the
calming influence and the ultimate plan-
ner. The maid of honor bracelet is one way
of thanking her for all she contributes. This
bracelet uses a combination of different
shapes of freshwater pearls. As there are so
many wonderful types of pearls available,
the range of possibilities is endless. Like the
bridesmaid's earrings, this bracelet incorporates the birthstone of the wearer (in this
case, aquamarine). Another unique aspect
of the design is inclusion of the birthstone of
the bride (sapphire in this case). This combination can serve as a reminder of the close-
ness of their bond.

MATERIALS

- eight 10-mm white coin pearls
- two 10-mm white square pearls
- five 8- × 20-mm white side-drilled stick pearls
- six 3-mm sapphire beads
- three 6-mm aquamarine briolettes
- one 4-mm sapphire blue Swarovski crystal
- 8" (20.3 cm) nylon coated stainless steel stringing wire Beadalon 49 Strand: 0.018" (0.46 mm) diameter
- 1" (2.5 cm) of sterling silver 3.2-mm long- and short-cable chain
- one 24-gauge (0.5 mm) 1½" (3.8 cm) sterling silver head pin
- one 14- × 10.6-mm figure-eight sterling silver lobster clasp
- two 2-mm sterling silver crimp beads
- flush-cut wire cutters
- crimping pliers
- round-nosed pliers
- flat-nosed pliers

Maid of Honor Bracelet

1 | Cut one piece of beading wire 8" (20.3 cm). The size of your bracelet can vary depending on the wrist size of the wearer; you need only to remember to have enough at the ends to comfortably finish off your crimp. This bracelet will measure 6½" (16.5 cm) with an additional chain for adjustment of 1" (2.5 cm).

2 | Slip one end of the beading wire through one of the crimp beads. Add the lobster clasp and slip the beading wire back through the crimp bead. Next **secure crimp** tightly, and trim off any excess wire flush against the crimp bead.

3 | Add pearls and sapphire beads in the following order: coin, square, coin, stick, sapphire, stick, sapphire, stick, coin.

4 | Now add the dominant design element. This is the part of the design that relates to the wearer's birth date. Add a sapphire bead, three aquamarine briolettes, and then another sapphire bead. Remember to pay attention to the size of the briolettes (see Jeweler's Tip for Coin Pearl and Aquamarine Bridesmaid Earrings, page 92).

5 | Add the remaining pearls and sapphire beads in the following order: coin, stick, coin, stick, coin, sapphire, square, sapphire, coin.

6 | Before finishing off the bracelet, make sure the pearls and stones are snug against each other without being so tight that they will not form a nice circle around the wearer's wrist.

7 | Finish off the bracelet by adding another crimp bead. Slip the end of the wire through the end of the 1" (2.5 cm) chain and back through the crimp bead. Next, **secure crimp** tightly and trim the wire flush with the end of the crimp bead.

8 | Take the head pin and slip on one coin pearl followed by the Swarovski crystal. Start a **wrap loop** on the end of the head pin, but before wrapping it around itself, slip the loop onto the end of the sterling silver chain. Complete the **wrap loop**.

Jeweler's Tip

Asymmetry can create a dynamic design when done properly. It is often more visually interesting than a static symmetrical pattern. It is important, however, to be careful to achieve an overall balance in the design. This balance is accomplished by making sure one side or area isn't visually heavier than the other. Alternate the type of pearls, but make sure they are approximately the same size. Designing this way may take some practice but will result in a creative and unusual piece of jewelry.

Variation

t here are infinite combinations of gemstones that can be used in the design of the maid of honor bracelet. If emerald is the birthstone of the bride and citrine is the birthstone of the maid of honor, the bracelet will have a completely different look. Also, different pearl shapes can be substituted. This bracelet is a symmetrical combination of eight coin pearls, two square pearls, and four stick pearls. As the square pearls are surrounding the central dominant element of the design, be careful to select two square pearls that closely match in luster and color. Make sure they are drilled exactly in the center.

Mother of the Bride Coin Pearl Necklace

The mother of the bride necklace uses similar white coin pearls that have been selected for the bride. It is a single-strand knotted necklace with a flattering length of 24" (61 cm). White coin pearls have a classic, elegant look. Accent stones are chosen to either complement the color of the mother of the bride's dress or represent her birthstone. This necklace will be cherished for years as a continuing reminder of the memorable event.

MATERIALS

- twenty-seven 14-mm white coin pearls
- thirty-six 4-mm iolite beads
- 42" (106.7 cm) of 0.0137" (0.348 mm) white silk thread
- one flexible stringing needle
- ½" (1.3 cm) of silver French wire
- one 14-mm sterling silver square toggle clasp
- Tri-Cord Knotter
- flush-cut wire cutters

Mother of the Bride Necklace

1| Make a knot at one end of the silk thread and attach a flexible needle to the other.

2| Thread three coin pearls, sliding them to the end of the silk thread.

3| Cut the ½" (1.3 cm) French wire in half, sliding half of it onto the needle, holding the French wire between your thumb and forefinger as it goes over the needle. Slide it down the thread until it is 2" (5.1 cm) above the three pearls.

4| Slide on the bar end of the toggle clasp and push down to the French wire.

5| Pass the needle through the closest pearl in the opposite direction, creating a loop of French wire snug against the pearl. Leave the 2" (5.1 cm) of space between this pearl and the next. Hand-tie a knot snug against the pearl.

6| Pass the needle through the next pearl and hand-tie another knot. Pass the needle through the final pearl; do not knot. Leave the short tail of thread with the knot in the end dangling from the strand of pearls. This will be trimmed at the end.

7| String the pearls and iolite beads in following order: three iolite beads, one coin pearl, three iolite beads, three coin pearls.

Repeat this pattern four times, followed by three iolite beads, one coin pearl, and three iolite beads. This will allow for three coin pearls to be added after knotting, finishing off the necklace.

8| Using the Tri-Cord Knotter, make a **secure knot** between each pearl and iolite bead. Refer to the techniques section, page 36, for a description on how to use the Tri-Cord Knotter.

9| String on the remaining three coin pearls.

10| Thread on the ¼" (6 mm) French wire, followed by the other end of the toggle clasp.

11| Pass the needle through the pearl closest to the French wire in the opposite direction, forming a loop of French wire next to the pearl. Make sure the three pearls are close together, allowing only for spaces for the hand-tied knots.

12| Hand-tie a knot around the thread in the first gap.

13| Pass the needle through the next pearl and hand-tie another knot around the thread in the second gap.

14| Pass the needle through the third coin pearl. Trim off the excess thread, pulling slightly on the thread to allow the thread to disappear within the pearl when it is trimmed.

15| Trim the excess thread at the other end in the same manner.

16| Place a very small drop of jeweler's cement on the hand-tied knots at both ends. Set aside until dry.

Jeweler's Tip

Take special care to achieve uniformity when knotting between the iolite beads. Any differentiation in the knots or any gaps between the knots will be more pronounced for the iolite beads. The smallness and sparkle of the gemstones accentuate imperfections.

Variation

peach coin pearls and ruby gemstones create an elegant, rich necklace. For this variation, the length is shorter, 20" (50.8 cm) and 14-karat gold is chosen to complement the warmth of the pearls. The color of the pearls may simply be decided based on personal preference or the decision might be driven by the birthstone colors of the bridal party. Ideally, the mother of the bride and the bride will have the same color of coin pearls, though their necklaces will be distinctly different.

Bride's Triple-Strand Necklace

A **pearl necklace has been the accepted**
standard for brides for many years. In fact,
it was approximately 3,000 years ago that
a father first gave his daughter the gift of
pearls on her wedding day. Pearls simply
epitomize the purity of the wedding tradition. The luxurious necklace shown here
is composed of three strands of white coin
pearls. The strands are hand-knotted, which
adds a timeless quality to the design. There
is an adage, "leave well enough alone," and
the biggest challenge for any designer is to
know when to stop. The perfection of these
white coin pearls dictated a conservative
approach to design. Nature, had in fact, done
most of the design work already. The smaller
11-mm pearls add scale and interest but
mainly reinforce the strong geometries of
this necklace.

MATERIALS

- fifty-eight 14-mm white coin pearls
- thirty-seven 11-mm white coin pearls
- two 8-mm 14-karat gold filigree beads
- three 42" (106.7 cm) segments of 0.0137" (0.348 mm) white silk thread
- three flexible stringing needles
- ½" (1.3 cm) of silver French wire
- one 10-mm 14-karat gold safety clasp with white cultured pearl
- Tri-Cord Knotter
- flush-cut wire cutters

Bride's Necklace

1. Make a knot at each end of the silk thread, leaving a tail of 9" (22.9 cm), and attach a flexible needle to the other.

2. For the first strand, thread twenty-three of the 14-mm coin pearls, sliding them to the end of the silk thread.

3. Using the Tri-Cord Knotter, make a **secure knot** between each pearl until all twenty-three have been knotted, including the knots at both ends of the pearl strand. Refer to the techniques section, page 36, for a description on how to use the Tri-Cord Knotter.

4. Repeat steps 2 and 3 for the other strand of 14-mm coin pearls.

5. For the third strand, thread thirty-one of the 11-mm coin pearls, sliding them to the end of the silk thread.

6. Using the Tri-Cord Knotter, make a **secure knot** between each pearl until all thirty-one have been knotted, including the knots at both ends of the pearl strand.

7. You are now ready to add the clasp to both sides of the triple-strand necklace.

8. On the ends of the strands with the needles attached, add three of the similar coin pearls to each strand (adding the 14-mm pearls to the strands with 14-mm pearls and the 11-mm pearls to the strand with the 11-mm pearls).

9. Thread all three needles through the 14-karat gold bead.

10. Cut the ½" (1.3 cm) French wire in half, sliding half of it onto the first needle, holding the French wire between your thumb and forefinger as it goes over the needle. Gently thread the second and third needle through the same French wire. This will require some patience and skill; remember to keep the French wire snuggly in between your thumb and forefinger. It will fit—use your flat-nosed pliers to grab onto the needle to ease it through. Slide the French wire down the threads until it is 2" (5.1 cm) above all the pearls.

Jeweler's Tip

Using a multistrand clasp for this project is the easiest way to finish off the necklace. With separate links to attach each thread, you avoid having to finesse three threads through one section of French wire. While I chose to describe a technique that is more challenging for the overachievers out there, a multistrand clasp is just as acceptable and can be just as elegant as the pearl clasp chosen. Simply follow steps 1–6, knotting the strands individually before you join them together on the clasp. This method allows you to work without having a cumbersome amount of material to pass through the loops as you are knotting. Attach each strand to the different links of the clasp using hand-tied knots, taking care to attach the same thread to the matching link on the other side of the clasp. Note your materials list must increase to add four additional sections of French wire.

11| Thread all three needles through one end of the clasp. Push the clasp down onto the French wire.

12| Pass all three needles through the 14-karat gold bead. Making sure the threads do not twist, pull the threads tightly so that the French wire forms a loop next to the 14-karat gold bead. Also, make sure the three pearls on each strand that will be hand-tied are close together, allowing only for spaces for the hand-tied knots.

13| Pass one needle through one of the pearls closest to the 14-karat gold bead in the opposite direction.

14| Hand-tie a knot around the thread in the first gap.

15| Pass the needle through the next pearl and hand-tie another knot around the thread in the second gap.

16| Pass the needle through the third coin pearl.

17| Repeat steps 13–16 for the two other strands.

18| Remove the three flexible needles and attach them to the other end of each strand.

19| Repeat steps 8–17 to add the hand-tied pearls and the clasp to the other end of the necklace.

20| Trim off all excess thread, pulling slightly on the thread to allow the thread to disappear within the pearl when it is trimmed.

21| Place a very small drop of jeweler's cement on the hand-tied knots at both ends. Set aside until dry.

Matching Pearl Stud Earrings

The bride's earrings must be as special as the bride. Cultured pearl stud earrings are selected for the post from which the coin pearls drop. Many styles of post earrings contain too much gold that overpower the simplicity and purity of the pearls. The elegant single stud cultured pearl complements the necklace and also represents the traditional choice of brides.

1| Slide the cultured pearl onto the mount pin of the post earring. If the pearl does not slip all the way onto the mount pin resting against the 14-karat gold cup, you will need to trim the excess. Remove the cultured pearl and trim the mount pin so that the pearl lies against the base of the 14-karat gold cup.

MATERIALS

- two 6-mm half-drilled white cultured pearls
- two 14-mm white coin pearls
- two 11-mm white coin pearls
- one pair of 14-karat gold 5-mm cup with mount pin post earrings with clutches
- two 24-gauge (0.5 mm) 2" (5.1 cm) 14-karat gold head pins
- jeweler's cement
- round-nosed pliers
- flat-nosed pliers
- flush-cut wire cutters

2| Using jeweler's cement, carefully add a drop of cement to the inside of the half-drilled pearl and slide back onto the mount pin. Set aside to dry.

3| Slide on one 14-mm coin pearl followed by one 11-mm coin pearl onto one head pin.

4| Use the flat- and round-nosed pliers to start a **simple loop**.

5| Attach the simple loop of the head pin onto the ring of the post earring and close the loop tightly.

6| Repeat the preceding steps to make another earring so that you have a matching pair.

CHAPTER 6

Gallery of Jewelry

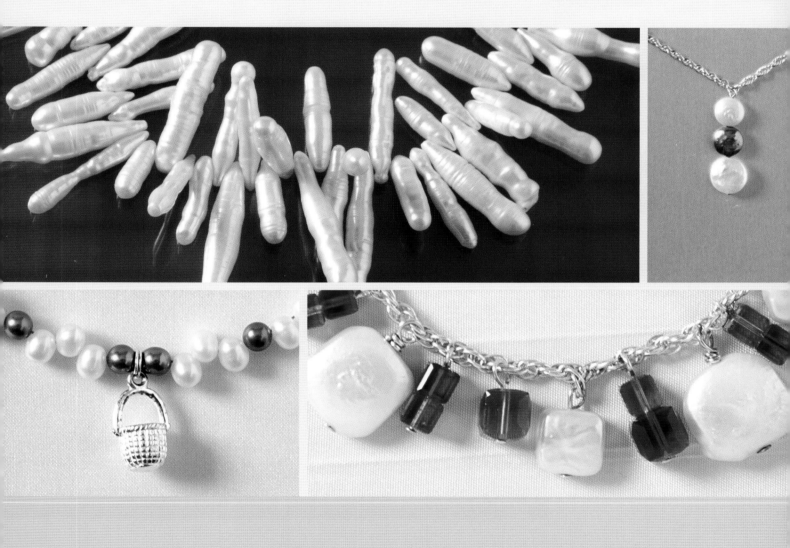

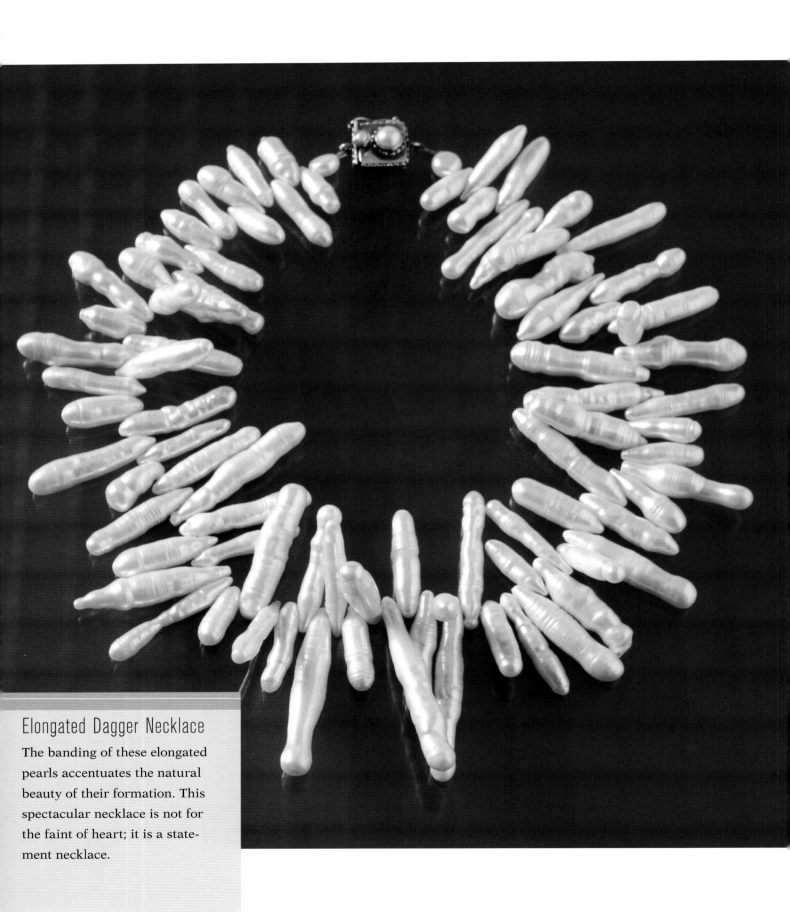

Elongated Dagger Necklace

The banding of these elongated pearls accentuates the natural beauty of their formation. This spectacular necklace is not for the faint of heart; it is a statement necklace.

Antique Venetian Trade Bead Choker

Peacock freshwater pearls complement, rather than dominate, the colors in the trade beads. This is a fun necklace to be worn as a choker.

Jangle Bracelet

This bracelet is a signature design. Rock crystal and white coin and stick freshwater pearls make it a perfect party bracelet year round.

Pearls with Rough Stone

The smooth iridescence of the coin drop pearls contrast beautifully with the rough stones of blue topaz. This necklace would be ideal for a special seaside celebration.

Basket of Eggs

This necklace is a lovely adornment for a young woman. The small, white teardrop pearls represent the eggs for the pendant basket.

Sweet Sixteen

The small, irregular rice freshwater pearls are complemented by aquamarine faceted teardrops. This is a perfect necklace for a prom, birthday, or bat mitzvah.

Simple Geometries

Sterling silver triple-rope chain dresses up this necklace, though it can be worn easily with a pair of blue jeans and a turtleneck. Simple freshwater shapes keep the design modern.

Party on a Wrist

Varying sizes of square freshwater pearls dance with red and pink Swarovski crystals. It's a perfect holiday bracelet.

Princess Necklace

White coin pearls
accentuated with
sapphires and
aquamarines evoke
a fairy-tale fit for a
princess.

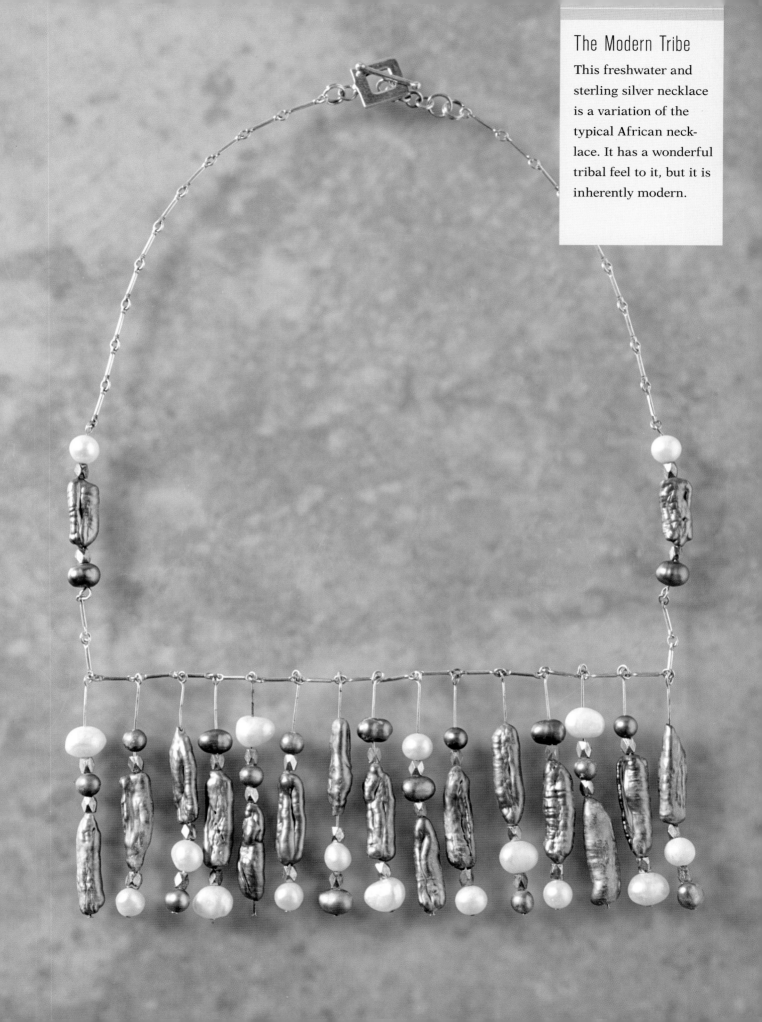

This freshwater and sterling silver necklace is a variation of the typical African necklace. It has a wonderful tribal feel to it, but it is inherently modern.

Cluster of Grapes

Small, gray freshwater potato pearls are attached to a simple French wire earring to form a cluster. There are many possible variations for this simple design.

Minimalist Dangle Earrings

Cleopatra would have loved these earrings. Side-drilled coin pearls support a small stack of gold and pearl. The length of the chain is a matter of personal preference.

Random Squares

Three different squares of material make up this warm, autumn necklace: Sponge coral is interspersed randomly with peach square freshwater pearls and square garnets.

Elegant Shapes Bracelet

The warm tones and high quality of the peach pearls make this an elegant bracelet.

Resources

The following list of resources is just enough to get you started. Local craft and bead stores provide the best hands-on resource for the beginning jewelry maker. They can help you locate the right material or tool or help you with a difficult technique. Whenever possible, support these individually owned enterprises. I have listed several international sources, but the Internet has made global boundaries less important. Have fun surfing the Internet, but always make sure you are dealing with a reputable business.

UNITED STATES

TAJ COMPANY
800.325.0825
www.tajcompany.com
Pearls and gemstones

EARTHSTONE
800.747.8088
www.earthstone.com
Pearls and gemstones

CK GEMS USA
212.683.0297
www.ckgemsusa.com
Pearls and gemstones

GOLDEN SEA ADVANCE, INC.
626.291.2277
www.goldenseaadv.com
Pearls and gemstones

A GRAIN OF SAND
704.660.3125
www.agrainofsand.com
Pearls and gemstones

RIO GRANDE
800.545.6566
www.riogrande.com
Large catalog of jewelry-related supplies
in all categories

STULLER, INC.
800.877.7777
www.stuller.com
Large catalog of jewelry-related supplies
in all categories

FIRE MOUNTAIN GEMS AND BEADS
800.355.2137
www.firemountaingems.com
Large catalog of jewelry-related supplies in all categories

HALSTEAD BEAD
800.528.0535
www.halsteadbead.com
Findings, metal, crystal, and other jewelry-related supplies

NINA DESIGNS
800.336.6462
www.ninadesigns.com
Clasps, Bali silver, and findings

STUDIO BABOO
434.244.2905
www.studiobaboo.com
My local bead store

MONSTERSLAYER
505.598.5322
www.monsterslayer.com
Large selection of pearls, beads, findings, and other jewelry-related supplies

SOUTH PACIFIC WHOLESALE CO.
800.338.2162
www.beading.com
Pearls and stone beads

TENNESSEE RIVER FRESHWATER PEARL FARM
800.225.7469
www.tennesseeriverpearls.com
Guided tours

INTERNATIONAL

CANADA

BEADFX
877.473.2323
www.beadfx.com
Pearls, beads, crystal, and findings

CANADIAN BEADING SUPPLY
800.291.6668
www.canbead.com
Large catalog of jewelry-related supplies

THE HOUSE OF ORANGE
250.544.0127
www.houseoforange.biz
Beads, crystal, and general jewelry-related supplies

ENGLAND

BEADGEMS
011.44.845.123.2743
www.beadgems.com
Pearls, beads, crystal, and findings

KERNOWCRAFTS ROCKS AND GEMS LIMITED
011.44.872.573.888
www.kernowcraft.com
Pearls, beads, and jewelry-related supplies

AUSTRALIA

SPACE TRADER BEADS
011.61.3.9534.6867
www.spacetrader.com.au
Pearls, beads, and other jewelry-related supplies

KATIE'S TREASURES
011.61.2.4956.3435
www.katiestreasures.com.au
Pearls, beads, and other jewelry-related supplies

About the Author

Nicole Noelle Sherman designs and creates jewelry in her studio in Free Union, Virginia. Her work grows out of a family tradition of art and architecture. Nicole's approach is to redefine the traditional and create unique pieces with careful attention to detail. Her jewelry designs center on the freshwater pearl. She believes that various shapes, sizes, and hues help dictate how each piece will evolve. Nicole's innovative designs offer a new look in freshwater pearl jewelry and reflect her love of organic materials and unusual form. Her work is available in galleries and fine jewelry stores in Virginia and New England and online through her website at www.nicolenoelle.com.

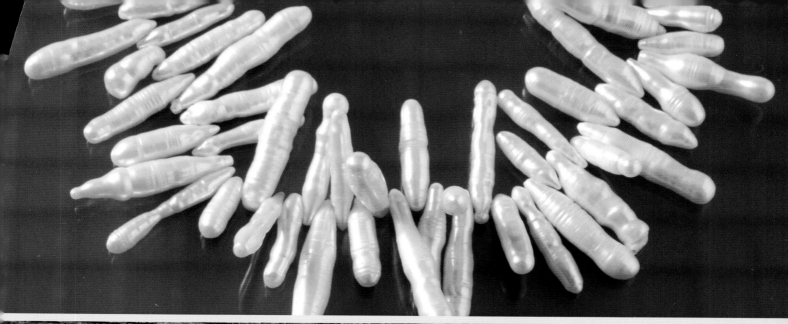

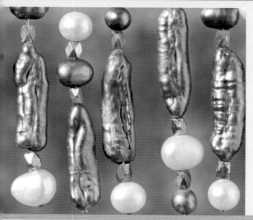

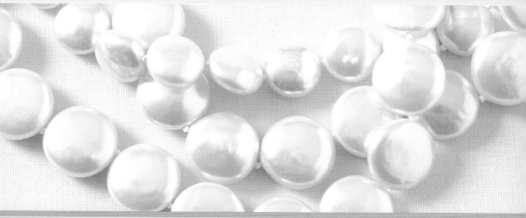

Acknowledgments

I would like to thank all the people at Quarry Books, especially acquisitions editor Mary Ann Hall and project manager and photo editor Betsy Gammons. Thank you, Mary Ann, for bringing the initial proposal to me and for guiding me throughout the entire process. Your insights and willingness to listen have been much appreciated. Thank you, Betsy, for your help along the way and your sense of humor; I look forward to our book signings. Thank you, Regina Grenier, art director, for your creativity and your flexibility. And, finally, thank you to the copy editor, photographer, and other professionals at Quarry who have made this project so rewarding.

In selling my work over the years, I have always had the pleasure of working with a fun and delightful group of people. In particular, thank you to Lyn Rushton, from Les Yeux du Monde. Lyn's fabulous gallery has been my home base and exclusive showcase in Charlottesville for years. Thank you Frannie Kansteiner at The Studio in Middleburg, Virginia and Heather Hartman at Hartman Jewelers in Warrenton, Virginia; you were the first in northern Virginia to carry my work. And thank you to Deb at Nahcotta, in Portsmouth, New Hampshire; Nahcotta showcases my other line of jewelry, Soft Hardwear. Thank you to all the wonderful people at the other galleries and fine jewelry stores in Virginia and New England. I look forward to many more years of creative collaboration.

Personally, I would be remiss if I didn't thank my husband for his unrelenting encouragement, even when my ideas were not as wonderful as I initially believed. Thank you also to my extended family and friends who have not only been supportive, but who have also been at times my best clients! And, finally, thank you to my mother, who taught me persistence and all the other important things.